Haunted Churches

& Sacred Sites

Spirits Among the Pews: Chilling Tales of the Holy and Haunted

By Lee Brickley

Copyright @ Lee Brickley 2023

Contents:

Introduction..5

The Phantom Choir of York Minster.......................................11

The Ghostly Monks of Mont Saint-Michel.............................17

The Weeping Lady of St. Nicholas Church............................23

The Whispers of Borley Rectory..29

The Vengeful Spirit of Lucedio Abbey...................................35

The Shadowy Figures of St. Louis Cathedral.......................43

The Haunting of St. Paul's Episcopal Church......................51

The Unearthly Hymns of St. Dunstan's Church...................57

The Crypt of Capuchin Catacombs...65

The Cursed Spirits of Leap Castle...71

The Ghostly Procession of St. Mary the Virgin....................77

The Enigmatic Entities of Sedlec Ossuary............................83

The Haunted Halls of St. Michan's Church...........................89

The Grieving Bride of St. Olaf's Church.................................95

The Sinister Shadows of St. Bartholomew-the-Great.......101

The Poltergeists of St. Andrew's on the Red......................107

The Watchful Spirits of St. Augustine's Monastery...........115

The Phantom Friars of Greyfriars Kirkyard..................121

The Crying Madonna of Syracuse..........................127

The Mysterious Apparitions of St. Mark's Basilica.........135

The Restless Dead of St. George's Church.................141

Afterword..147

Introduction

In the hallowed halls of ancient churches and sacred sites, where countless souls have sought solace, peace, and redemption, an inexplicable darkness lingers. Behind the serene facades of these magnificent structures lie centuries of secrets, tragedies, and supernatural phenomena. In "Haunted Churches and Sacred Sites: Spirits Among the Pews," we embark on a chilling journey to explore the mysterious, eerie, and sometimes terrifying tales of the holy and haunted.

As we traverse the globe, delving into the shadowy corners of history, we will encounter spirits that defy explanation and stories that send shivers down the spine. From the whispering vaults of the Borley Rectory in England to the enigmatic apparitions of St. Mark's Basilica in Venice, we will uncover the truth behind the tales of the supernatural that have echoed through time. These stories are not for the faint of heart, but for those who seek to unravel the mysteries of the world beyond our understanding.

Our journey begins with the Phantom Choir of York Minster, an English cathedral steeped in history and shrouded in spectral legends. As the sun sets and darkness envelops the grand structure, visitors have reported hearing the ethereal sounds of a ghostly choir, accompanied by fleeting glimpses of spectral figures. The origins of these haunting encounters remain a mystery, but the stories persist, drawing curious souls from around the world.

Across the English Channel, on the iconic French island of Mont Saint-Michel, we delve into the haunting history of the ghostly monks who are said to roam the abbey's hallowed halls. Cloaked in darkness, these hooded apparitions have been sighted by numerous witnesses, their silent presence an eerie reminder of the ancient monastery's storied past.

As we venture further into the heart of Europe, we find ourselves in the ancient city of Prague, home to the tragic tale of the Weeping Lady of St. Nicholas Church. Her ghostly form, forever mourning a lost love, is said to haunt the church's shadowy corners, her anguished cries echoing through the night. The story of her heartbreak is a chilling testament to the powerful emotions that bind us to the world, even in death.

Our exploration of the haunted and the holy leads us to the shores of the Mediterranean, where the Crypt of Capuchin Catacombs in Sicily houses a macabre collection of mummified remains. This site, steeped in death and decay, has been the setting for numerous supernatural occurrences, with witnesses reporting unexplained sounds and movements among the catacombs' eerie inhabitants.

As we leave the Mediterranean behind, we journey to the Emerald Isle, home to the Cursed Spirits of Leap Castle. Within the crumbling walls of Ireland's most haunted fortress, we will uncover a violent history that has given rise to sinister hauntings and spine-chilling encounters with the restless dead. From the infamous "Bloody Chapel" to the castle's labyrinthine corridors, the spirits that linger within Leap Castle offer a chilling insight into the darker side of Ireland's past.

Our voyage continues to the historic city of Oxford, where the Ghostly Procession of St. Mary the Virgin Church offers a glimpse into the spectral world that lies just beyond our perception. The church, rich in history and architectural beauty, has borne witness to countless souls throughout the centuries, some of whom are said to still wander its hallowed grounds, locked in an eternal dance with the shadows.

As we delve deeper into the mysteries of haunted churches and sacred sites, our journey takes us to the heart of the Czech Republic, where the chilling legends of Sedlec Ossuary – the "Bone Church" – await. This macabre site, adorned with the skeletal remains of thousands, is said to be haunted by enigmatic entities that defy explanation. The chilling atmosphere within the ossuary, where bones and skulls are intricately arranged in an eerie display, is said to be a breeding ground for supernatural occurrences, leaving visitors with an unsettling sense of unease as they navigate the labyrinthine corridors lined with the remains of the departed.

Our exploration of the haunted and the holy takes us next to the ancient Dublin landmark of St. Michan's Church. Beneath its peaceful exterior lie the eerie vaults, where mummified remains rest in eternal slumber. Visitors have reported feeling an unsettling presence within the crypts, as if the restless spirits of the long-dead watch from the shadows, waiting for their stories to be told.

Farther east, we discover the tragic love story that haunts Estonia's oldest church, St. Olaf's. The Grieving Bride, forever mourning her lost love, is said to appear as a ghostly figure that roams the church's grounds. The tale of her heartbreak and the ghostly apparitions that linger at St. Olaf's serve as a poignant reminder of the enduring power of love, even beyond the grave.

As we return to the heart of London, we investigate the sinister shadows and malevolent entities that are said to dwell within the mediaeval priory of St. Bartholomew-the-Great. The unexplained phenomena that have been reported within its hallowed walls bear witness to a dark history that refuses to be forgotten, leaving a lingering sense of unease in the air.

In the remote reaches of Manitoba, Canada, we uncover the mysterious happenings and ghostly tales that surround St. Andrew's on the Red. The spirits that haunt this historic church are said to make their presence known through poltergeist activity, leaving those who dare to venture within its walls questioning the limits of their own understanding.

Our journey through the world of haunted churches and sacred sites comes to a close at St. Augustine's Monastery in Germany. Within the ancient abbey, visitors have reported eerie encounters and unexplained paranormal activity, as if the watchful spirits of those who once dwelt within the monastery's walls continue to keep a vigilant eye on their sacred home.

As we have traversed the globe, uncovering chilling tales and mysterious phenomena that defy explanation, it is evident that the spirits among the pews offer a unique window into the world beyond our comprehension. From the ethereal echoes of phantom choirs to the tragic tales of heartbreak and loss, the stories that emerge from these hallowed halls serve as a haunting reminder of the thin veil that separates our world from the unknown. In "Haunted Churches and Sacred Sites: Spirits Among the Pews," we have only just begun to scratch the surface of the mysteries that lie within these ancient sanctuaries, but for those brave enough to delve into the shadows, a world of chilling encounters and supernatural intrigue awaits.

The Phantom Choir of York Minster

Nestled in the heart of the ancient city of York, York Minster stands as a beacon of spiritual solace and a testament to the remarkable skill and artistry of the craftsmen who built it. With its soaring Gothic spires, exquisite stained glass windows, and magnificent mediaeval architecture, this awe-inspiring cathedral has been a centre of worship, pilgrimage, and learning for over a millennium. However, as the sun sinks below the horizon and the streets of York are bathed in darkness, a more chilling atmosphere descends upon the hallowed halls of this sacred sanctuary. For it is within these ancient walls that visitors have reported encountering the ethereal sounds of a ghostly choir and fleeting glimpses of spectral figures, whose origins remain shrouded in mystery.

To better understand the haunting legends that surround York Minster, it is necessary to delve into the cathedral's storied past.

The origins of the Minster can be traced back to the year 627 AD, when a wooden structure was erected on the site to house the baptism of Edwin, the King of Northumbria. Over the centuries that followed, the humble church was gradually replaced by increasingly grandiose buildings, culminating in the construction of the current Gothic edifice, which was completed in the 15th century. With its towering central tower, intricate stone carvings, and exquisite craftsmanship, York Minster is a masterpiece of ecclesiastical architecture, which has borne witness to countless souls throughout the ages.

As we delve deeper into the cathedral's history, we begin to uncover the roots of the haunting tales that have become inextricably entwined with its hallowed walls. The legends of the Phantom Choir of York Minster are said to have originated in the 16th century, during the turbulent reign of Henry VIII. As the king sought to break with the Catholic Church and establish the Church of England, the once-thriving monastic communities of the country found themselves in the crosshairs of his wrath. The dissolution of the monasteries saw the destruction of countless sacred sites, and the lives of the monks and nuns who resided within them were torn asunder. At York Minster, the choir – which had been a central pillar of the cathedral's musical and liturgical traditions – was disbanded in the wake of these tumultuous events, leaving a profound sense of loss that would echo through the centuries.

It is said that the ghostly sounds of the Phantom Choir began to be heard soon after the dissolution, as if the spirits of the long-departed monks and nuns were seeking to reclaim their sacred space. The haunting melodies, which are often accompanied by flickering candlelight and a sudden drop in temperature, have been experienced by numerous witnesses over the years. The eerie, disembodied voices seem to emanate from deep within the cathedral's vaults, echoing through the shadowy corners and ancient stone passageways.

One particularly chilling account comes from a local historian, who was conducting research within the Minster's library late one evening. As the clock struck midnight, he suddenly became aware of a haunting choral melody, which seemed to be coming from the choir stalls below. Descending the winding stone staircase, he found the cathedral bathed in an ethereal glow, with spectral figures clad in the robes of mediaeval monks and nuns standing at attention in the stalls. As he watched in stunned silence, the ghostly choir continued to perform their celestial hymn, before fading from sight as the final note reverberated through the hallowed halls.

Another eyewitness, a vicar who had come to York Minster to attend a conference, reported a similarly unnerving encounter. While wandering the cathedral's labyrinthine passageways after the day's events, the vicar found himself drawn to the sound of ethereal singing, which seemed to emanate from the depths of the Minster. As he followed the haunting melody, he found himself in the Chapter House, where the ghostly choir appeared before him in a shimmering display of spectral light. The apparitions sang with an otherworldly beauty that left the vicar entranced, before vanishing as suddenly as they had appeared.

The Phantom Choir of York Minster has continued to captivate the imaginations of visitors and locals alike, with numerous accounts of ghostly encounters and mysterious happenings adding to the cathedral's mystique. Some theories suggest that the spectral choir is composed of the spirits of those who once served the Minster in life, their souls forever bound to the sacred space they held so dear. Others believe that the haunting melodies are a manifestation of the collective memories of the thousands who have passed through the cathedral's hallowed halls, the music an echo of the joy, sorrow, and devotion that have been etched into its ancient stones.

As we continue to explore the mysterious sounds and spectral figures haunting York Minster, it becomes clear that the Phantom Choir is just one facet of the cathedral's rich tapestry of supernatural phenomena. Other reports detail encounters with ghostly monks who glide silently through the shadows, their faces obscured by the hoods of their habits. Some visitors have even claimed to see the specter of a long-dead archbishop, his regal robes trailing behind him as he walks the aisles, forever tending to his spiritual flock.

One particularly chilling account comes from a group of tourists who had ventured into the cathedral's crypt, hoping to catch a glimpse of the legendary Phantom Choir. As they descended the narrow stone staircase, they suddenly found themselves engulfed in an unnatural darkness, as if the very walls were closing in around them. The air grew heavy and oppressive, and the faint sound of weeping could be heard echoing through the gloom. The terrified group quickly retreated from the crypt, convinced that they had encountered a malevolent presence that did not wish to be disturbed.

In recent years, the legends of the Phantom Choir of York Minster have continued to draw curious souls from around the world, each seeking to unravel the mysteries that lie within the cathedral's ancient walls. Some come in search of the ghostly choir, hoping to hear the haunting melodies that have echoed through the centuries. Others are drawn to the cathedral's rich history and its myriad tales of spectral figures, restless spirits, and unexplained phenomena. For those who are brave enough to delve into the shadows, the hallowed halls of York Minster offer a chilling journey into the unknown, where the veil between our world and the next is stretched thin, and the spirits of the past continue to walk among us.

As we leave the storied grounds of York Minster, we are left to ponder the enigmatic origins of the Phantom Choir and the spectral figures that are said to haunt the cathedral's ancient walls. Are these ghostly encounters simply the product of overactive imaginations, fueled by centuries of folklore and whispered tales? Or do they offer a tantalising glimpse into a world that lies just beyond our understanding, a realm where the spirits of the past continue to dwell, forever bound to the hallowed halls that they once called home? The answers to these questions remain as elusive as the ethereal figures that haunt the shadows of York Minster, leaving us to wonder what other mysteries may lie hidden within the sacred sanctuaries of our haunted churches and sacred sites.

The Ghostly Monks of Mont Saint-Michel

Standing proud off the coast of Normandy, France, Mont Saint-Michel is a breathtaking sight to behold. A majestic Gothic-style abbey, perched atop a tidal island, it is surrounded by the crashing waves of the Atlantic Ocean. The island has a rich history, dating back to the 8th century, when it was first established as a religious sanctuary. Today, it is a UNESCO World Heritage site, attracting millions of visitors each year who come to marvel at its stunning architecture and beautiful surroundings. But Mont Saint-Michel also has a darker side, steeped in mysterious legends and chilling ghost stories. As the sun sets and shadows creep across the island, a sense of unease descends upon the ancient abbey, as if the spirits of the past still roam its hallowed halls.

The history of Mont Saint-Michel can be traced back to the year 708, when the Bishop of Avranches, Aubert, received a vision of the Archangel Michael instructing him to build a church atop the rocky island. At first, Aubert was hesitant to follow the divine command, but after the Archangel's repeated insistence, he finally acquiesced. Thus, the first church on Mont Saint-Michel was constructed in honour of the Archangel. Over the centuries, the site continued to grow, with a Benedictine abbey and a fortified village being added in the following years. The island's strategic location and formidable defences made it a stronghold during times of conflict, notably resisting multiple sieges during the Hundred Years' War.

As the centuries passed, Mont Saint-Michel's importance as a religious centre began to wane, and by the time of the French Revolution in 1789, the once-thriving abbey had been reduced to a mere handful of monks. The island's fortunes took a darker turn still when it was repurposed as a prison during the Revolution, housing many political dissidents and other unfortunate souls within its cold, unforgiving walls. It was not until 1863 that the prison was finally closed, and Mont Saint-Michel began its slow transformation into the tourist destination it is today.

The ghostly tales that surround Mont Saint-Michel are as old as the island itself, with countless generations of visitors and residents alike sharing chilling accounts of spectral encounters and otherworldly presences. Perhaps the most famous of these stories are those of the ghostly monks who are said to haunt the ancient abbey. Dressed in dark, hooded robes, these spectral figures are often seen wandering the island's narrow streets or gliding silently through the abbey's dimly lit corridors.

One of the earliest recorded sightings of these ghostly monks dates back to the 17th century when a traveller named Claude Mauger claimed to have encountered a group of hooded figures during his visit to Mont Saint-Michel. Mauger was staying in the village inn when he was awoken in the dead of night by the sound of footsteps outside his window. Curious, he peered through the glass and was astonished to see a procession of dark, hooded figures making their way slowly towards the abbey. As he watched, the ghostly monks seemed to vanish into the shadows, leaving no trace of their passing.

Throughout the centuries, there have been many more accounts of similar eerie encounters. One particularly chilling tale is that of a young woman named Marguerite, who visited Mont Saint-Michel in the late 19th century. Marguerite was exploring the abbey's cloisters when she suddenly found herself enveloped in a cold, chilling sensation. Turning around, she came face to face with a tall, hooded figure, standing silently in the shadows. The apparition had a pale, ghostly visage that seemed to stare straight through her. Paralyzed with fear, Marguerite could do nothing but watch as the spectral monk glided away, disappearing as it passed through the ancient stone walls.

More recent eyewitness accounts have also surfaced, testifying to the enduring presence of these ghostly monks. In 1987, a group of tourists visiting Mont Saint-Michel reported seeing a hooded figure standing in the abbey's choir, bathed in a pale, otherworldly glow. As they approached, the figure seemed to dissolve into the air, leaving behind an unsettling sense of unease.

Another notable encounter occurred in 2004 when a young couple on their honeymoon decided to explore the abbey after hours. As they made their way through the darkened hallways, they were startled by the sudden appearance of a hooded figure, standing silently at the end of a dimly lit corridor. Before they could react, the spectral monk glided away, disappearing into the darkness as if it had never been there at all.

Theories abound as to the identity and purpose of these ghostly monks. Some believe that they are the spirits of the early

Benedictine monks who once inhabited Mont Saint-Michel, forever bound to the abbey by their devotion and piety. Others suggest that they may be the tormented souls of prisoners who suffered and died within the island's cold, unforgiving walls during its time as a prison. Still, others speculate that they may represent a psychic imprint of the past, a lingering echo of the countless souls who once walked the hallowed halls of Mont Saint-Michel.

Whatever the truth may be, the tales of the ghostly monks of Mont Saint-Michel have become an intrinsic part of the island's rich tapestry of history and folklore. As the shadows lengthen and night descends upon the ancient abbey, the line between the realms of the living and the dead seems to blur, and the spirits of the past continue to make their presence felt in this iconic French island.

The Weeping Lady of St. Nicholas Church

In the heart of Prague's picturesque Lesser Town, with its cobblestone streets and Baroque architecture, stands the magnificent St. Nicholas Church. Completed in 1755, the church is considered one of the finest examples of High Baroque architecture in Central Europe. It was designed by Christoph Dientzenhofer and his son, Kilian Ignaz Dientzenhofer, who were among the most renowned architects of their time. The church boasts a grandiose dome, a soaring bell tower, and an intricately decorated interior adorned with frescoes and sculptures by the leading artists of the Baroque era.

Throughout the centuries, St. Nicholas Church has been a place of worship and solace for countless souls. However, amidst the splendour of its sacred halls, a tragic tale of love and loss has given rise to a chilling paranormal phenomenon – the Weeping Lady. This ghostly figure, her tearful countenance a testament to her enduring heartbreak, is said to haunt the church's shadowy corners, her mournful cries echoing through the night.

The story of the Weeping Lady dates back to the 18th century when the church was still under construction. A young woman named Isabella was betrothed to a local stonemason, Antonín, who was working on the construction of the church. The couple was deeply in love, and their impending nuptials were the talk of the town. However, their happiness was not to last, as fate had other plans in store for the young lovers.

One fateful day, Antonín was working on the construction of the church's bell tower when a tragic accident occurred. A heavy stone fell from the tower, striking Antonín and killing him instantly. Devastated by the loss of her beloved, Isabella was inconsolable. In her grief, she would visit the church every day, weeping at the foot of the tower where Antonín had lost his life. As the years passed, her grief only deepened, and she became a ghostly presence within the church, her wails of sorrow a haunting reminder of her tragic loss.

The legend of the Weeping Lady has persisted over the centuries, as visitors to St. Nicholas Church have reported encountering the sorrowful spirit. Her apparition is described as a young woman dressed in a flowing white gown, her long hair cascading over her tear-streaked face. Witnesses have reported hearing her heart-rending cries, as well as feeling a cold chill in the air when in her presence.

One notable account comes from a local historian named Jakub, who visited the church in the late 19th century. As he was examining the intricate carvings within the bell tower, he suddenly heard the sound of weeping. Startled, he looked around and saw the apparition of a young woman, her face contorted in anguish as tears streamed down her cheeks. The vision was so vivid and haunting that Jakub, a self-proclaimed sceptic, was compelled to delve into the history of St. Nicholas Church, eventually uncovering the tragic tale of Isabella and Antonín.

Another account comes from a group of tourists who visited the church in the early 20th century. As they were exploring the church's interior, they were startled by the sound of a woman sobbing. They searched for the source of the sound but could find no one. It was only later, when they learned of the legend of the Weeping Lady, that they realised they had encountered the ghostly presence of Isabella herself.

In more recent times, a visiting priest from Italy, Father

Giovanni, experienced an encounter with the Weeping Lady that left a profound impact on him. While staying at the church to attend a conference, Father Giovanni awoke in the middle of the night to the sound of heart-wrenching sobs. He initially thought that a parishioner was in distress and made his way to the church's main hall to offer assistance. Upon entering, he saw a figure dressed in white, her face buried in her hands as she wept. As he approached, she slowly lifted her tear-streaked face, and he realised that this was no ordinary woman but the spirit of Isabella herself. Deeply moved by the encounter, Father Giovanni later shared his experience with his fellow priests, adding further testimony to the enduring legend of the Weeping Lady.

Although the tragic tale of the Weeping Lady is rooted in the past, it continues to captivate the hearts and minds of those who visit St. Nicholas Church. Some see the story as a cautionary tale about the power of grief and the importance of finding solace in the face of tragedy. Others view the ghostly apparition of Isabella as a reminder of the enduring bond between two lovers, transcending the boundaries of time and death.

In the hallowed halls of St. Nicholas Church, where the echoes of the past reverberate through its sacred spaces, the Weeping

Lady remains an enigmatic presence. Her heartrending cries, forever bound to the ancient walls of the church, are a chilling testament to the power of love, loss, and the human spirit. As the legend of the Weeping Lady endures, it serves as a haunting reminder that, even within the sacred confines of a church, the spectre of human tragedy and the mysteries of the paranormal continue to captivate and intrigue those who dare to delve into the shadows of history.

The Whispers of Borley Rectory

In the quiet village of Borley, nestled in the picturesque countryside of Essex, lies a once-grand Victorian mansion with a chilling past. Borley Rectory, with its imposing façade and stately architecture, has long been a subject of fascination and fear for those who dare to delve into its haunted history. As we turn our attention to this enigmatic site, we will explore the tales of paranormal phenomena and ghostly encounters that have earned it the title of England's most haunted rectory.

The rectory's story begins in the late 19th century, when it was constructed on the grounds of a mediaeval monastery. Completed in 1863, the rectory was initially home to the Reverend Henry Dawson Ellis Bull and his family. It was during the Bull family's residence that the first reports of unexplained occurrences began to emerge. The family claimed to have heard disembodied footsteps echoing throughout the house, and mysterious figures were said to have been seen lurking in the shadows. One of the most intriguing tales from this time involved the sighting of a ghostly nun, who was believed to have wandered the grounds, her mournful gaze fixed on the rectory.

The history of the haunting at Borley Rectory seems to be rooted in the dark past of the monastery that once stood on the site. Legend has it that a 13th-century monk from the monastery had fallen in love with a beautiful nun from a nearby convent. Their forbidden love affair was discovered, and they were both executed as a result – the monk was hanged, and the nun was bricked up alive within the walls of the convent. The tragic tale of the doomed lovers is thought to be the source of the spectral nun and the eerie atmosphere that permeates the rectory.

As the years passed, the stories of hauntings and unexplained events continued to swirl around Borley Rectory. In 1930, the Reverend Guy Eric Smith and his wife took up residence in the rectory, and they soon discovered that they were not alone. Mysterious whispers were heard emanating from the walls, and ghostly figures were seen wandering the grounds. Desperate for answers, the Smiths contacted the Daily Mirror, which in turn brought the case to the attention of famed paranormal investigator Harry Price. Price's initial investigation into Borley

Rectory would mark the beginning of a decades-long fascination with the site, and his findings would cement its reputation as a hotbed of supernatural activity.

During Price's investigation, he and his team of researchers were witness to a variety of inexplicable phenomena. They experienced sudden drops in temperature, heard unexplained footsteps and knocking sounds, and saw objects move seemingly of their own accord. Price also made contact with a spirit through a planchette session, during which the spirit claimed to be a French nun named Marie Lairre, who had been murdered and buried in the cellar of the rectory. This chilling revelation only served to deepen the mystery surrounding Borley Rectory, and it became a focal point for paranormal enthusiasts and ghost hunters alike.

One of the most chilling encounters at Borley Rectory took place during a séance conducted by Price and his team in 1937. As they sat in the darkness, they were suddenly confronted by the apparition of a terrifying figure. The entity, which appeared to be a tall, hooded man with a gaunt, skeletal face, moved silently through the room before vanishing into the shadows. The chilling encounter was a turning point for Price and his team, who became more determined than ever to unravel the secrets of Borley Rectory.

Despite the mounting evidence of paranormal activity, not everyone was convinced of the rectory's haunted nature. Sceptics questioned the veracity of the accounts and suggested that the events could be attributed to natural phenomena or even the power of suggestion. However, those who had experienced the chilling occurrences firsthand maintained that there was something otherworldly at work within the walls of Borley Rectory.

In 1939, disaster struck when a fire broke out in the rectory, causing extensive damage and rendering the building uninhabitable. The fire's origin remains a mystery, with some speculating that it was the result of supernatural forces, while others believe it was an act of arson. In the years that followed, Borley Rectory fell into disrepair and was eventually demolished in 1944. Despite its destruction, the land on which the rectory once stood continues to be a source of fascination and fear for those who believe in the paranormal.

The eerie history of Borley Rectory has left a lasting impression on the village of Borley and the wider world of paranormal research. Eyewitness accounts of ghostly encounters and chilling occurrences at the rectory have been recorded in books and articles, preserving the memory of this enigmatic site for generations to come. One such account comes from a local resident who, while walking near the site of the rectory in the 1960s, claimed to have seen a ghostly figure of a woman in white, believed to be the spectral nun, walking across the grounds before disappearing into the night.

Another more recent account comes from a group of paranormal investigators who, in the early 2000s, visited the remains of Borley Rectory's foundations to conduct a nighttime investigation. During their visit, they reported hearing unexplained footsteps, disembodied voices, and the sensation of being watched by unseen eyes. The group also captured a number of unexplained images on their cameras, which they believe to be evidence of lingering supernatural activity at the site.

As we delve into the chilling tales and mysterious events surrounding Borley Rectory, it is impossible to ignore the lingering sense of unease that seems to permeate the very air around the site. While sceptics may dismiss the accounts of paranormal activity as mere flights of fancy or the result of overactive imaginations, the sheer number of eyewitness accounts and the compelling nature of the experiences they describe cannot be easily dismissed.

In the end, the true nature of the phenomena that occurred at Borley Rectory may never be fully understood. But as we explore the dark corners of haunted churches and sacred sites around the world, it is clear that the whispers of Borley Rectory continue to echo through time, a chilling reminder of the mysteries that lie just beyond the edges of our perception. Whether the result of supernatural forces, tragic history, or the power of the human mind, the haunting of Borley Rectory remains a captivating and spine-chilling tale that will endure for generations to come.

The Vengeful Spirit of Lucedio Abbey

In the stunning region of Piedmont, Italy, the imposing structure of Lucedio Abbey casts a long shadow over the surrounding countryside. Constructed in 1123 by Cistercian monks, the abbey was once a thriving centre of religious devotion and agricultural innovation. Today, it stands as a testament to the passage of time, its once-magnificent halls now filled with whispers of tragedy and ghostly encounters.

The history of Lucedio Abbey is inextricably intertwined with the rise and fall of religious power throughout Italy. Founded by the Cistercians, a monastic order known for their devotion to austerity, humility, and manual labour, the abbey quickly established itself as a beacon of spiritual enlightenment in the region. The monks of Lucedio were responsible for introducing the cultivation of rice to the Piedmont area, an innovation that would have far-reaching effects on the local economy and culture.

As the centuries passed, however, the abbey's fortunes began to wane. Corruption and moral decay set in, and rumours of unspeakable acts taking place within the monastery's walls began to spread like wildfire. The once-devout order had become a breeding ground for sin and debauchery, and the abbey itself seemed to take on a malevolent presence.

It was during this dark period in the abbey's history that the first reports of paranormal activity began to surface. Visitors to the monastery spoke of a pervasive sense of dread that seemed to hang in the air, as though the very walls were bearing witness to the unspeakable deeds that had been committed within. Others claimed to have seen ghostly apparitions, dark figures that appeared to be in great pain, wandering the abbey's halls and chambers.

Over time, the stories of hauntings at Lucedio Abbey grew more frequent and more disturbing. The ghostly figures seen by visitors were no longer just the tormented souls of monks but also included the spectres of young girls who had been rumoured to have been subjected to heinous acts by the monks during the abbey's darkest days.

One of the most chilling tales associated with Lucedio Abbey is that of a vengeful spirit, said to be the embodiment of the dark energy that had seeped into the very foundations of the monastery. This malevolent entity is believed to be responsible for the many strange occurrences that have plagued the abbey over the centuries.

The spirit is said to be that of a former abbot, who had been executed for his role in the corruption and depravity that had overtaken the once-holy institution. His ghost is said to have returned to the abbey to exact vengeance on those responsible for his death, as well as any who dared to set foot on the cursed ground.

The legends of the vengeful spirit of Lucedio Abbey have been passed down through the generations, inspiring fear and fascination in equal measure. Some have dismissed the tales as mere folklore, the product of overactive imaginations and the passage of time. Others, however, maintain that there is a kernel of truth to the stories, and that the abbey is indeed haunted by the restless spirits of those who suffered and died within its walls.

The accounts of paranormal encounters at Lucedio Abbey are as varied as they are chilling. Some visitors have reported experiencing a sudden drop in temperature, accompanied by an overwhelming sense of dread, as they enter the monastery's ancient halls. Others have described hearing the distant, anguished cries of tormented souls, echoing through the air as if carried on the wind.

One of the most compelling eyewitness accounts comes from a local woman named Maria, who claims to have encountered the vengeful spirit of the former abbot during a visit to the abbey in the late 20th century. As she explored the crumbling structure, she was overcome by a sudden feeling of unease. The air seemed to grow colder, and an inexplicable sense of dread began to grip her. As she turned a corner into a dimly lit chamber, she was confronted by the ghastly apparition of a man dressed in tattered monastic robes, his eyes filled with rage and despair. The spirit stared at her for a moment before vanishing into the shadows, leaving Maria shaken to her core.

Another visitor, a historian named Luca, had ventured to Lucedio Abbey to study the architectural features of the mediaeval structure. As he examined an ancient fresco on one of the abbey's walls, he was startled by the sound of footsteps approaching from behind. He turned to see a hooded figure in monastic robes, walking slowly towards him. The figure's face was obscured by the shadows of the hood, but Luca could see the unmistakable glint of malice in the entity's eyes. As the figure drew closer, it suddenly vanished, leaving the historian in a state of shock and disbelief.

In more recent years, paranormal investigators have been drawn to Lucedio Abbey, eager to uncover the truth behind the legends that have swirled around the site for centuries. Armed with the latest technology and a keen sense of curiosity, these intrepid explorers have ventured into the depths of the haunted monastery, hoping to capture evidence of the supernatural.

During one such investigation, a team of paranormal researchers set up their equipment in the abbey's chapel, the room that was rumoured to be the epicentre of the spiritual activity. As they monitored their instruments, the temperature in the room began to drop, and a chilling breeze seemed to materialise out of thin air. The team's electronic devices began to malfunction, their screens flickering and batteries draining at an alarming rate.

As the investigators attempted to make sense of the strange phenomena, a loud, guttural growl echoed through the chamber, emanating from a dark corner of the room. The team's cameras captured a shadowy figure, barely visible to the naked eye, that seemed to manifest and disappear in the blink of an eye. The investigators left the abbey that night shaken, but more determined than ever to unlock the mysteries that lay within its walls.

The tales of paranormal activity at Lucedio Abbey continue to attract visitors from around the world, each drawn to the haunted site in search of answers, adventure, or perhaps just a glimpse of the unknown. Some come away disappointed, convinced that the legends of the vengeful spirit are nothing more than fanciful tales spun by the local populace. Others, however, leave the abbey with a newfound respect for the power of the supernatural, their own chilling encounters etched into their memories.

The legacy of Lucedio Abbey, once a bastion of religious piety and devotion, has been forever tainted by the darkness that took root within its walls. The tragic history of the monastery, marred by corruption and cruelty, has given rise to a series of supernatural encounters that continue to defy explanation. As the stories of the vengeful spirit and the tormented souls that haunt the abbey persist, the ruins of the once-great monastery stand as a chilling reminder of the human capacity for both good and evil, and the thin line that separates the two.

In our exploration of haunted churches and sacred sites, Lucedio Abbey offers a fascinating and chilling insight into the world of the supernatural. The legends of the vengeful spirit and the haunted halls of the monastery serve as a cautionary tale, a stark reminder of the consequences of our actions and the echoes they leave behind.

The Shadowy Figures of St. Louis Cathedral

In the heart of New Orleans' vibrant and bustling French Quarter stands a majestic structure that has endured centuries of change and upheaval. St. Louis Cathedral, an iconic symbol of the city's unique blend of cultures, is a testament to the steadfast faith of its congregation and the power of spiritual unity. Yet, beneath the facade of this awe-inspiring edifice lies a hidden world of restless spirits and haunting tales that have echoed through the generations.

The history of St. Louis Cathedral is as rich and multifaceted as the city it calls home. First established in 1718 by French settlers and dedicated to King Louis IX of France, the church was originally a modest wooden structure, built to serve the spiritual needs of the burgeoning colony. In the years that followed, the church would undergo a series of transformations, each iteration reflecting the shifting tides of history that ebbed and flowed through the streets of New Orleans.

In 1727, a devastating fire swept through the city, consuming the original wooden structure in its fiery embrace. Determined to rebuild, the congregation constructed a new edifice, this time crafted from brick and adorned with a steeple. However, fate had other plans for the beleaguered church. In 1788, another fire ravaged the French Quarter, leaving much of the city in ruins, including the newly built brick cathedral. It was not until 1794, under the direction of Spanish architect Don Gilberto Guillemard, that the current iteration of St. Louis Cathedral took shape, a stunning example of Spanish Colonial architecture that has remained an enduring symbol of the city's resilience and spirit.

The storied past of St. Louis Cathedral has left an indelible mark on the hallowed grounds it occupies. The spirits that linger within its walls and surrounding cemetery have tales to tell, stories that speak of tragedy, sorrow, and the enduring strength of the human spirit. Over the years, countless witnesses have come forward with accounts of paranormal encounters and inexplicable occurrences that defy rational explanation. Some believe that these spectral denizens are the remnants of the church's tumultuous history, while others see them as a testament to the powerful emotions and spiritual energy that have been woven into the very fabric of the cathedral.

One of the most enduring and chilling tales associated with St. Louis Cathedral involves the enigmatic figure of Father Antonio de Sedella, better known as Père Antoine. A Spanish Capuchin priest, Père Antoine arrived in New Orleans in 1774 and quickly became an integral part of the city's spiritual life. He was a tireless advocate for the downtrodden and a champion of the rights of the enslaved, earning the love and respect of the people he served.

Upon his death in 1829, Père Antoine was interred within the walls of the cathedral, his final resting place nestled within the very heart of the church he had so faithfully served. Yet, it seems that even in death, the spirit of Père Antoine remains a vigilant guardian of his beloved city. Countless visitors have reported encountering the ghostly visage of the priest, clad in his distinctive Capuchin robe, wandering the grounds of the cathedral and the surrounding streets. Some have even claimed to have been touched by his gentle hand, a comforting reminder of the eternal love and compassion he embodied in life.

Another spectral figure that has been frequently sighted within the hallowed halls of St. Louis Cathedral is that of a young woman named Marie. The tragic story of Marie's life is one of heartbreak and betrayal. As a young woman, Marie fell deeply in love with a dashing young sailor, and the couple pledged their undying devotion to one another. However, fate had other plans for the star-crossed lovers. The sailor, called away to sea, left Marie behind, promising to return and make her his wife. Yet, as the months turned to years, Marie's once unwavering faith in her lover's return began to wane.

In her despair, Marie sought solace within the walls of St. Louis Cathedral, praying fervently for a sign that her love had not been in vain. One fateful day, as she knelt before the altar, her prayers were answered in the most heartrending manner. The doors of the cathedral swung open, and a funeral procession entered, bearing the earthly remains of her long-lost sailor. Overwhelmed by grief, Marie's spirit shattered, and she died shortly thereafter, her heart broken beyond repair.

Ever since that tragic day, the ghostly figure of Marie has been spotted within the cathedral, her mournful gaze forever searching for the love that was cruelly snatched away. Some visitors have reported hearing her soft, sorrowful sobs echoing through the church, a haunting testament to the enduring power of love and the depths of human heartache.

In addition to the ghostly residents who seem to be inextricably linked to the cathedral's storied past, there are also numerous accounts of more enigmatic spirits and unexplained phenomena that have been reported within its hallowed halls. One such occurrence is the appearance of mysterious, shadowy figures that seem to materialise out of the darkness, only to vanish just as suddenly as they appeared.

These elusive entities have been sighted by numerous visitors, often lurking in the dimly lit corners of the cathedral, just beyond the reach of the flickering candlelight. While the origins of these shadowy figures remain a mystery, some have speculated that they could be the remnants of souls who found solace within the church during their time of need, or perhaps even the spirits of those interred within the adjacent cemetery, drawn to the spiritual energy that permeates the cathedral's walls.

Among the many accounts of paranormal encounters within St. Louis Cathedral, one in particular stands out for its eerie and inexplicable nature. In the late hours of the night, when the cathedral lies shrouded in darkness, witnesses have reported hearing the chilling sound of a disembodied voice, softly reciting prayers and hymns in an ancient, long-forgotten language. The source of this spectral voice remains a mystery, as no physical presence has ever been detected in conjunction with the haunting sounds.

The ghostly tales and chilling encounters that surround St. Louis Cathedral offer a fascinating glimpse into the hidden world that exists just beyond the limits of our perception. The spirits that dwell within its walls and the unexplained phenomena that defy rational explanation serve as a haunting reminder of the enduring power of faith, love, and the human spirit.

As we conclude our exploration of the shadowy figures and restless spirits that haunt St. Louis Cathedral, it is evident that the church's storied past has left an indelible mark on the hallowed grounds it occupies. The tales of heartbreak, tragedy, and enduring strength that have echoed through the centuries serve as a testament to the powerful emotions and spiritual energy that have been woven into the very fabric of the cathedral.

The haunting stories and eerie encounters that have become an intrinsic part of the cathedral's history serve as a fascinating reminder of the mysteries that lie hidden within these ancient sanctuaries. For those brave enough to delve into the shadows, a world of chilling encounters and supernatural intrigue awaits, offering a unique window into a realm that exists just beyond our comprehension.

The Haunting of St. Paul's Episcopal Church

Tucked away at the southernmost point of the continental United States lies the charming and historic island of Key West. Steeped in history and enveloped in an air of mystery, this tropical paradise is not only a treasure trove of beautiful scenery, but it also harbours its share of spine-chilling tales. Among the various tales of the supernatural and inexplicable, one of the most compelling is the haunting of St. Paul's Episcopal Church.

Founded in 1832, St. Paul's Episcopal Church holds the distinction of being the oldest church in South Florida. Its storied past is one of resilience and rebirth, having been rebuilt no less than four times in its nearly two centuries of existence. The first three churches succumbed to the ravages of hurricanes and fire, with the current Gothic Revival style structure standing proudly on the corner of Duval Street and Eaton Street since 1919.

Designed by architect J. H. Weddell, the church stands as a testament to the enduring faith of the congregation and the resilience of the human spirit.

But within the walls of this sacred sanctuary, there are whispers of an otherworldly presence that seems to defy explanation. From the unexplained sounds of disembodied voices to sightings of ghostly apparitions, the tales of paranormal activity at St. Paul's Episcopal Church have captured the imagination of believers and sceptics alike.

The origins of the haunting can be traced back to the tumultuous history of the church itself. In its early years, St. Paul's served as a beacon of hope and solace for the burgeoning community of Key West. The congregation played an instrumental role in the island's development, providing not only spiritual guidance but also support for civic and charitable causes. Over the years, the church bore witness to countless baptisms, weddings, and funerals, each leaving an indelible mark on the fabric of the community.

One of the most tragic events in the church's history occurred in 1889 when a fire broke out in the sanctuary, claiming the lives of several parishioners who were trapped inside. It is believed that the spirits of those who perished in the blaze continue to linger within the hallowed halls, their presence manifesting in a variety of inexplicable phenomena.

Eyewitness accounts of paranormal activity at St. Paul's Episcopal Church are as varied as they are chilling. One of the most frequently reported occurrences involves the ghostly figure of a woman dressed in Victorian-era clothing. She is said to appear near the church's baptismal font, often accompanied by the faint scent of roses. The identity of this spectral figure remains a mystery, but some speculate that she may be the spirit of a grieving mother who lost her child in the tragic fire of 1889.

Another recurring manifestation involves the unexplained sounds of footsteps echoing through the empty church. Visitors and staff alike have reported hearing the distinct sound of someone walking through the aisles and pews, despite no one being present. This phenomenon has been attributed to the restless spirit of a former priest who is said to have perished in one of the hurricanes that devastated the church in the 19th century.

Perhaps the most unsettling account of paranormal activity at St. Paul's involves the sighting of a ghostly apparition in the church's bell tower. This figure, described as a shadowy presence with an air of malevolence, is said to watch over the church from its lofty perch. The true nature of this entity is shrouded in mystery, with some speculating that it may be the spirit of a long-forgotten parishioner who met an untimely end within the church's walls.

But the tales of the supernatural at St. Paul's Episcopal Church are not limited to ghostly apparitions and unexplained noises. Reports of poltergeist activity have also been documented, with objects inexplicably moving or disappearing, only to reappear in entirely different locations. Some believe that these occurrences are the work of mischievous spirits, seeking to make their presence known to those who dare to enter the church's hallowed halls.

One particularly chilling account involves a former church organist who, while practising late one night, was startled by the sudden appearance of a ghostly figure seated in the pews. The figure, which appeared to be a woman dressed in period clothing, seemed to listen intently as the organist played, her expression one of profound sadness. As the organist finished their piece, the figure vanished, leaving no trace of her presence.

The haunting of St. Paul's Episcopal Church has attracted the attention of paranormal investigators and enthusiasts alike, each seeking to unravel the mysteries that lie within its storied walls. Many have attempted to communicate with the spirits that are said to inhabit the church, with varying degrees of success. Some have reported receiving intelligent responses through the use of electronic voice phenomena (EVP) recordings, while others have captured inexplicable images and anomalies on film and video.

But despite the numerous attempts to uncover the truth behind the paranormal activity at St. Paul's Episcopal Church, the true nature of the haunting remains a mystery. Some argue that the church's turbulent history has left an indelible mark on the building itself, causing the residual energy of past events to manifest in the form of ghostly phenomena. Others suggest that the spirits of those who once worshipped within the church's walls have chosen to remain, their eternal devotion to their faith anchoring them to the world of the living.

Regardless of the origins of the haunting, the tales of the supernatural at St. Paul's Episcopal Church serve as a fascinating glimpse into the unknown, a chilling reminder that there are still mysteries that defy our understanding. As visitors continue to flock to this historic Key West landmark, drawn by its beauty and the eerie allure of its ghostly inhabitants, the spirits of St. Paul's Episcopal Church continue to weave their enigmatic tales, beckoning those brave enough to venture into the shadows in search of answers.

The haunting of St. Paul's Episcopal Church is a testament to the power of the human spirit and the enduring nature of faith. As the church continues to thrive, providing solace and guidance to its congregation, the spirits that dwell within its walls remain a captivating and enigmatic presence. Whether they are echoes of the past, seeking to share their stories with the living, or guardians of the sacred space, watching over the church from the realm of the unknown, one thing is certain: the tales of the haunting of St. Paul's Episcopal Church will continue to captivate and intrigue.

The Unearthly Hymns of St. Dunstan's Church

The St. Dunstan-in-the-West Church, located on Fleet Street in London, has been a sanctuary for the faithful and a spiritual landmark for nearly a thousand years. Its history can be traced back to the early 10th century when it was founded as a Benedictine priory. Over the centuries, the church has been rebuilt and renovated multiple times, most notably in the 19th century when it was reconstructed in the neo-Gothic style under the supervision of architect John Shaw Jr.

Despite the numerous alterations and restorations that have taken place within its walls, the church remains steadfast in its mission, providing solace and spiritual guidance to its parishioners. However, beneath the surface of this revered place of worship lies an eerie history that has led many to believe that St. Dunstan's is haunted by ghostly presences and otherworldly manifestations.

The legends of hauntings at St. Dunstan's Church have their origins in the complex and often turbulent history of the church itself. Throughout the centuries, the church has borne witness to numerous upheavals and transformations, both in its physical structure and in its role within the community. During the 16th century, the church was the site of an infamous incident involving the execution of several monks who had been accused of treason. These executions took place within the churchyard, and the traumatic events have left an indelible mark on the collective memory of those who worship at St. Dunstan's.

Another significant event in the history of the church's hauntings took place in the 19th century when the church was being rebuilt. During the extensive renovations, it is believed that several graves were disturbed, and the remains of the deceased were inadvertently removed from their final resting places. This disturbance of the dead is thought to have contributed to the increased paranormal activity within the church, as the spirits of the displaced souls seek restitution for the desecration of their graves.

Numerous accounts of unexplained phenomena have been reported within the hallowed halls of St. Dunstan's Church, with the most notable being the eerie sounds of ghostly organ music and disembodied voices. These auditory manifestations are said to occur primarily in the dead of night when the church is empty and silent, leaving those who experience the phenomena with a lingering sense of unease.

One of the most compelling eyewitness accounts of these spectral sounds comes from a local organist who was practising late one evening within the church. As he played the haunting melodies of his chosen pieces, he became aware of a subtle, yet unmistakable, accompaniment to his performance. The ghostly music seemed to emanate from the depths of the church itself, reverberating through the vast, shadowy space with an ethereal quality that both intrigued and unnerved the organist. Despite his initial apprehension, the organist continued to play, and the spectral accompaniment persisted, seemingly harmonising with his own performance.

The organist's experience is far from an isolated incident, with many visitors to the church reporting similar encounters with the ghostly music and voices. On several occasions, witnesses have claimed to hear the strains of a long-lost hymn being sung by an invisible choir. This spectral choir is often described as being comprised of both male and female voices, which blend together in perfect harmony to create an otherworldly and hauntingly beautiful sound. The ethereal music is said to fill the church, its echoes bouncing off the ancient stone walls and reverberating through the hallowed space.

The disembodied voices that have been reported at St. Dunstan's Church are not limited to the mysterious choir. Many visitors have also claimed to hear whispered conversations and faint, distant laughter echoing through the empty corridors and chambers of the church. These ghostly voices seem to emanate from unseen sources, lending an eerie and unsettling quality to the atmosphere within the church's walls.

One such account comes from a parishioner who had stayed behind after a Sunday service to light a candle in memory of a loved one. As she knelt in silent prayer, she became aware of a hushed conversation taking place somewhere within the church. Straining to hear the words, she realised that the voices were speaking in a language she could not understand. The murmured exchange continued for several minutes before fading away into silence, leaving the parishioner with a profound sense of wonder and disquiet.

Another chilling account of disembodied voices at St. Dunstan's Church comes from a group of visitors who were exploring the church's crypt. As they descended the narrow, winding staircase into the subterranean chamber, they began to hear faint laughter echoing through the dank, dimly lit space. The laughter seemed to surround them, as if emanating from multiple sources hidden within the shadows. As they continued to explore the crypt, the laughter persisted, accompanied by the unmistakable sound of footsteps and the rustling of unseen figures moving through the darkness. The group, unnerved by the eerie sounds and sensations, quickly made their way back to the safety of the church above.

Many theories have been put forth in an attempt to explain the mysterious phenomena that seem to pervade the ancient walls of St. Dunstan's Church. Some believe that the ghostly organ music and disembodied voices are the spirits of long-deceased monks and clergy members who once served within the church, their ethereal presence a testament to their enduring devotion to their faith.

Others speculate that the spectral sounds and voices may be the echoes of past tragedies and traumas that have taken place within the church's walls, the residual energy of these events imprinting itself upon the very fabric of the building. The haunting tales of executed monks and disturbed graves lend credence to this theory, suggesting that the church may be a repository for the emotions and energies of its tumultuous past.

A more scientific explanation for the ghostly phenomena at St. Dunstan's Church posits that the unique acoustics and architecture of the building may be responsible for the auditory manifestations experienced by visitors. The soaring vaulted ceilings, intricate stone carvings, and labyrinthine layout of the church could potentially create an environment in which sounds are distorted and amplified, leading to the perception of otherworldly music and voices.

Regardless of the true origins of the unearthly hymns and disembodied voices at St. Dunstan's Church, the accounts of these spectral encounters continue to captivate and intrigue both believers and sceptics alike. The church's long and storied history, coupled with the eerie and unexplained phenomena that seem to haunt its halls, has cemented its place in the annals of haunted churches and sacred sites around the world.

As the sun sets over London and the shadows lengthen within the ancient walls of St. Dunstan-in-the-West, the air within the church seems to hum with an energy that defies explanation. The ghostly organ music and disembodied voices that reverberate through the hallowed space serve as an eerie reminder that, within the sacred confines of this historic church, the line between the spiritual and the supernatural is not always clear. For those who dare to venture within its walls after dark, the haunting melodies and whispered conversations of St. Dunstan's Church may forever remain.

The Crypt of Capuchin Catacombs

The island of Sicily, steeped in history and rich with cultural heritage, has long been a place where tales of the supernatural and the macabre abound. One such place, known for its eerie atmosphere and chilling encounters with the otherworldly, is the Crypt of Capuchin Catacombs. Located in the city of Palermo, this subterranean network of catacombs has been the final resting place for thousands of the deceased, their bodies preserved in a haunting display of mummification that has captivated and disturbed visitors for centuries.

The history of the Capuchin Catacombs dates back to the late 16th century when the Capuchin friars, an offshoot of the Franciscan order, established their monastery on this site. As the friars required a burial space for their deceased brethren, they began the process of excavating the underground tunnels that would eventually become the catacombs. The first friar to be interred within the catacombs was Brother Silvestro of Gubbio, who was buried there in 1599. His body, which was exhumed in 1625 to make room for more burials, was found to be remarkably well-preserved, with the friars attributing this phenomenon to the unique environmental conditions within the catacombs.

As word of the miraculous preservation of Brother Silvestro's body spread, the catacombs became an increasingly popular burial site for not only the friars but also for the wealthy and prominent citizens of Palermo. The process of mummification was refined over time, with the bodies being drained of fluids, washed with vinegar, and then left to dry in sealed rooms for approximately one year. Once the drying process was complete, the bodies would be dressed in their finest attire and placed within the catacombs, often posed in lifelike positions that mimicked their former lives.

Today, the Capuchin Catacombs are home to over 8,000 mummified remains, including men, women, and children, as well as several notable figures, such as the Baroque painter Pietro Novelli and the esteemed surgeon Salvatore Manzella. Among the most famous and haunting inhabitants of the catacombs is Rosalia Lombardo, a two-year-old girl who died in

1920. Her body, impeccably preserved and encased within a glass coffin, is often referred to as the "Sleeping Beauty" due to her lifelike appearance and the enduring sense of innocence that surrounds her.

While the macabre spectacle of the mummified remains within the Capuchin Catacombs is enough to send shivers down the spine of even the most stoic visitor, the site has also been the setting for numerous reports of supernatural activity. From disembodied whispers and footsteps echoing through the darkened corridors to sudden drops in temperature and unexplained feelings of being watched, the catacombs have long been a place where the inexplicable seems to lurk just out of sight.

One particularly chilling account comes from a local historian named Antonio, who had been conducting research within the catacombs late one evening. As he studied the inscriptions on the walls, he suddenly felt a cold hand touch his shoulder, causing him to jump in fright. When he turned around, he found himself face-to-face with a spectre of a hooded figure, its eyes hollow and staring. As Antonio stumbled back in terror, the figure vanished into the darkness, leaving him shaken and questioning the nature of the encounter.

Another tale comes from a group of students who had been visiting the catacombs on a guided tour. As they made their way through the eerie maze of tunnels, the students were captivated by the sight of the mummified remains, each one telling its own silent story of a life long past. As they reached a particularly darkened corner of the catacombs, one of the students, named Maria, claimed to see a shadowy figure darting between the rows of mummies. Intrigued, the group ventured further into the darkness, their flashlights casting eerie shadows upon the walls.

As they continued to follow the fleeting figure, the students were suddenly overcome by a sense of unease, as if they were being watched by unseen eyes. The air around them grew colder, and the whispers of disembodied voices filled the air. Despite their growing fear, the students pressed on, determined to uncover the source of the mysterious figure.

As they reached a dead-end within the catacombs, the shadowy figure appeared before them once more, this time taking the form of a woman dressed in tattered, 19th-century clothing. Her face, gaunt and pale, seemed to be filled with a deep sadness that seemed to emanate from her very being. As the students stared in shock and disbelief, the spectral woman reached out towards them, her eyes pleading for understanding. But before any of them could react, she vanished, leaving the students with a haunting memory that would stay with them for the rest of their lives.

The Capuchin Catacombs, with their chilling atmosphere and macabre inhabitants, have long been a place where the supernatural seems to manifest itself in ways that are as mysterious as they are terrifying. Some believe that the spirits of the deceased, bound to their mortal remains through the process of mummification, are unable to find peace in the afterlife, leaving them trapped within the confines of the catacombs. Others speculate that the catacombs, with their darkened corridors and eerie silence, are a magnet for otherworldly entities, drawn to the site by the potent energy that surrounds it.

No matter what the reasons behind the supernatural occurrences within the Capuchin Catacombs might be, one thing is certain: the site remains a haunting testament to the power of death and the unknown that lies beyond our understanding. For those who dare to venture into the catacombs, the chilling encounters and eerie whispers that echo through the darkness serve as a reminder that, in the presence of the mummified dead, we are never truly alone.

As the tales of the Capuchin Catacombs continue to captivate and unsettle those who hear them, the site stands as a stark reminder of our own mortality and the enduring fascination with the mysteries of the afterlife. From the enigmatic Rosalia Lombardo to the spectral figures that are said to roam the catacombs' darkened corridors, the stories of the supernatural and the macabre that surround this Sicilian site are as chilling as they are intriguing. In the hallowed halls of the Crypt of Capuchin Catacombs, where the mummified dead stand silent vigil, we find ourselves confronted with the eternal question of what lies beyond the veil of death, and whether the spirits that are said to dwell within these ancient tunnels have a message for us from the other side. For those who dare to explore the eerie world of the Capuchin Catacombs, the answers to these questions may forever remain shrouded in darkness, but the haunting encounters and chilling tales that emerge from this macabre site continue to captivate and terrify in equal measure.

The Cursed Spirits of Leap Castle

The Irish countryside, known for its breathtaking landscapes and ancient legends, is home to a fortress with a chilling past. Leap Castle, a foreboding structure that looms over the rolling green hills of County Offaly, has earned a sinister reputation as Ireland's most haunted castle. The malevolent forces that are said to dwell within its walls have given rise to a host of spine-chilling tales and eerie encounters, offering a glimpse into the dark underbelly of Ireland's storied past.

Leap Castle's history is steeped in violence and bloodshed. Originally built by the O'Bannon clan in the late 13th century, the fortress was later seized by their kinsmen, the fearsome O'Carroll clan. The O'Carrolls, known for their ruthlessness and cunning, ruled over the region with an iron fist, sparking countless feuds and skirmishes with neighbouring clans. The castle's strategic location, perched atop a rocky outcrop, provided its inhabitants with an ideal vantage point for observing approaching enemies, while its labyrinthine corridors and imposing walls offered ample protection from attack.

Throughout its turbulent history, Leap Castle has borne witness to countless acts of treachery and brutality, as its occupants waged a relentless battle for power and control. The infamous "Bloody Chapel," a grim reminder of the castle's violent past, is the site of one of its most gruesome episodes. According to legend, the castle's chieftain, Teige O'Carroll, desired to consolidate his power by eliminating his rivals within the clan. In a horrifying act of treachery, he burst into the chapel during a family Mass, slaughtering his own brother, a priest, on the altar. The blood-stained chapel, now in ruins, has become synonymous with the dark history of Leap Castle and is said to be the epicentre of its sinister hauntings.

The violent deeds that have taken place within the castle's walls are believed to have given rise to a host of restless spirits, forever trapped within the fortress's crumbling confines. One such entity, known as the "Elemental," is said to be a malevolent force that has haunted Leap Castle for centuries. Described as a terrifying, half-human, half-animal creature, the Elemental is said to emit an overwhelming stench of rot and decay, striking fear into the hearts of those who encounter it. Some believe that the Elemental was summoned by the O'Carrolls to protect their stronghold and to inflict suffering upon their enemies. Others theorise that the creature is a manifestation of the castle's dark history, a physical embodiment of the evil that has permeated its walls.

Over the years, numerous eyewitness accounts of encounters with the Elemental have emerged, each more chilling than the last. One such encounter took place in the early 20th century, when the castle's then-owner, a man named Jonathan Charles Darby, and his wife, Mildred, claimed to have come face to face with the sinister entity. Mildred, a prolific writer, documented her experiences with the Elemental in a series of letters, describing the creature as a grotesque, shadowy figure that loomed over her bed, its icy breath filling the room with a foul stench. In another account, a visitor to the castle reported feeling a sudden, overwhelming sense of dread, followed by the sensation of icy fingers gripping her throat, as if the Elemental sought to choke the life from her.

In addition to the Elemental, Leap Castle is said to be haunted by the spirits of the countless souls who met their untimely ends within its walls. Among these restless spirits are the ghosts of two young girls, who are believed to have lived in the castle during the 17th century. According to local lore, the sisters met a tragic fate when they fell to their deaths from the castle's battlements, their anguished cries echoing through the night as they plunged into the darkness below. Today, visitors to Leap Castle have reported witnessing the ethereal forms of the two girls, their laughter echoing through the corridors as they playfully chase one another through the fortress's shadowy recesses.

Another chilling tale that has become inextricably linked with Leap Castle's haunted history is that of the "Red Lady." Clad in a flowing crimson gown, the Red Lady is said to wander the castle's halls, clutching a dagger tightly to her chest. Legend has it that she was a young woman who was held captive by the O'Carroll clan and subjected to unspeakable horrors. After giving birth to a child, she is said to have taken her own life with the very dagger that she now brandishes in her ghostly form. Her spirit, unable to find peace in the afterlife, is forever condemned to roam the castle, reliving the torment of her final days.

Leap Castle's sinister reputation has attracted paranormal investigators and curious visitors from around the world, each eager to catch a glimpse of the restless spirits that are said to haunt its crumbling walls. One such investigator, the renowned psychic medium, Sybil Leek, conducted a séance at the castle in the 1970s, during which she claimed to have made contact with several of its ghostly inhabitants. During the séance, Leek reported being overwhelmed by the sheer number of spirits that seemed to be clamouring for her attention, each eager to communicate their stories and seek solace in the living world.

In more recent years, Leap Castle has been the subject of numerous television programs and documentaries, each seeking to shed light on the chilling tales that surround the fortress and its ghostly inhabitants. In one particularly chilling episode, a film crew captured what appeared to be the spectral figure of a man, clad in period clothing, as he wandered through the castle's dimly lit corridors. The footage, which has been analysed by experts in the field, has left many baffled, unable to provide a rational explanation for the eerie apparition.

Despite the sinister reputation that has come to define Leap Castle, it remains a popular tourist attraction, drawing visitors from far and wide who are eager to explore its dark history and experience the thrill of a close encounter with the supernatural. The castle's current owner, musician Sean Ryan, has devoted himself to the restoration and preservation of the fortress, ensuring that its legacy lives on for future generations to discover. Under Ryan's stewardship, Leap Castle has opened its doors to the public, offering guided tours that delve into its haunted past and shed light on the chilling tales that have become the stuff of legend.

For those who dare to venture within Leap Castle's imposing walls, the promise of an encounter with the unknown awaits. As visitors wander through the fortress's labyrinthine corridors and crumbling chambers, the spirits of the past seem to linger in the shadows, forever bound to the fortress that they once called home. From the blood-soaked stones of the Bloody Chapel to the eerie whispers that echo through the castle's dimly lit halls, Leap Castle offers a chilling insight into the darker side of Ireland's past, and a tantalising glimpse into the realm of the supernatural that lies just beyond the edge of our understanding. The Cursed Spirits of Leap Castle, with their tragic stories and spine-chilling encounters, serve as a haunting testament to the enduring power of the supernatural and the mysteries that continue to defy explanation.

The Ghostly Procession of St. Mary the Virgin

In the city of Oxford, England, renowned for its prestigious university and scholarly pursuits, there exists a church that has stood the test of time, its roots reaching back to the late 11th century. St. Mary the Virgin, a stunning architectural masterpiece with its intricate carvings, soaring spire, and striking stained-glass windows, has long been a beacon of spirituality for the local community and visitors alike. Within its ancient walls, the church has been a silent witness to countless souls who have passed through seeking solace, wisdom, and redemption. Yet, unbeknownst to many, St. Mary the Virgin harbours a dark secret that emerges when night falls and the shadows grow long.

The history of St. Mary the Virgin Church is rich and fascinating, its origins deeply entwined with the development of Oxford University. In fact, St. Mary's holds the distinction of being the university's first home, with its original purpose being to serve as the centre for teaching and administration. Over the centuries, the church has undergone numerous restorations and extensions, leaving a magnificent blend of architectural styles that range from the early English Gothic to the Perpendicular period. Among its many claims to fame, St. Mary's boasts the presence of the ornate University Pulpit, from which John Wesley, the founder of Methodism, delivered his sermons to rapt audiences in the 18th century. The church's rich tapestry of history and architectural beauty has made it a must-see destination for visitors to Oxford, drawing admirers from all corners of the world.

However, it is not merely the church's storied past and breathtaking architecture that has captured the imagination of those who pass through its doors. As the sun dips below the horizon and the last vestiges of daylight fade, an eerie transformation takes place within the hallowed grounds of St. Mary the Virgin. For centuries, locals and visitors alike have whispered of strange occurrences and spectral apparitions that emerge from the shadows, their presence a haunting reminder of the church's long history and the countless souls who have traversed its sacred pathways.

The most infamous of these supernatural phenomena is the Ghostly Procession, a chilling spectacle that has been reported by numerous eyewitnesses over the years. Described as a sombre parade of spectral figures dressed in mediaeval garb, the Ghostly Procession is said to materialise within the church and make its way through the nave, its participants bearing an air of solemnity and purpose. The figures are often described as being ethereal, their forms translucent and barely visible, as if they are the remnants of a long-forgotten past, clinging to the edges of the present.

The origins of the Ghostly Procession remain a mystery, with no definitive historical event or tragedy tied to the phenomenon. Some have speculated that the spectral parade may be linked to an ancient ritual or religious ceremony that took place within the church's walls, the participants forever bound to reenact their roles in the great drama of the afterlife. Others have suggested that the figures may be the spirits of individuals who were once buried within the church, their presence a testament to the enduring connection between the living and the dead.

Whatever the reason behind the Ghostly Procession, the eyewitness accounts of the haunting phenomenon are as chilling as they are intriguing. One such account comes from a local historian who, while conducting research in the church's archives late one evening, found himself confronted by the spectral figures as they emerged from the darkness and silently filed past him, their faces etched with an expression of profound sadness.

Another account, dating back to the early 20th century, comes from a young woman who had come to the church seeking solace after the tragic loss of her fiancé during World War I. As she knelt in quiet contemplation, she suddenly became aware of a faint, otherworldly glow emanating from the chancel. Looking up, she saw the ghostly figures materializing before her eyes, their translucent forms flickering in the dim light. She later described the experience as both haunting and strangely comforting, as if the spectral figures were fellow mourners, bound together in their shared grief.

Yet another account comes from a group of university students who, on a dare, decided to spend the night within the church's walls. As the hours passed and the shadows grew longer, the students began to notice strange sounds echoing through the nave, like the rustling of fabric and the soft murmuring of voices. Then, without warning, the Ghostly Procession materialised before them, the spectral figures moving solemnly through the church, their faces shrouded in darkness. The students, terrified by the sight, fled the church, vowing never to return.

Over the years, countless individuals have come forward with their own stories of encounters with the Ghostly Procession, each account adding to the growing body of evidence that something otherworldly exists within the hallowed halls of St. Mary the Virgin. While some dismiss these tales as mere flights of fancy, the sheer volume of eyewitness reports and the chilling consistency of the descriptions lend credence to the notion that the church may indeed be haunted by spectral figures from a long-forgotten past.

The haunting tales of St. Mary the Virgin's Ghostly Procession have captivated the imagination of paranormal enthusiasts, historians, and the general public alike, drawing many to the church in the hopes of catching a glimpse of the otherworldly spectacle. For some, the experience is one of fascination and wonder, an opportunity to peer into the unknown and gain a deeper understanding of the mysteries that lie beyond our comprehension. For others, the Ghostly Procession serves as a chilling reminder of the inescapable connection between the living and the dead, a manifestation of the eternal dance between light and darkness, and the enduring power of human emotion and spirituality.

In the end, the true nature of the Ghostly Procession of St. Mary the Virgin may forever remain a mystery, shrouded in the mists of time and the shadows of the unknown. However, one thing is certain: the haunting tales of the church's spectral visitors continue to capture the imagination of those who hear them, leaving an indelible mark on the annals of history and the human psyche.

The Enigmatic Entities of Sedlec Ossuary

Few places on Earth manage to capture the imagination, evoke a sense of awe, and elicit a shiver of fear quite like the Sedlec Ossuary. Located in the heart of the Czech Republic, the small Roman Catholic chapel – often referred to as the "Bone Church" – houses the skeletal remains of an estimated 40,000 to 70,000 individuals. Their bones have been artfully arranged into intricate, mesmerising, and macabre displays that fill the ossuary with an atmosphere that is as chilling as it is fascinating.

The history of the Sedlec Ossuary dates back to 1278 when the King of Bohemia sent the Abbot of Sedlec, Henry, on a diplomatic mission to the Holy Land. Upon his return, the Abbot brought back a small amount of soil from Golgotha, the site of Jesus Christ's crucifixion, and sprinkled it on the grounds of the Sedlec Cemetery. The holy soil transformed the cemetery into a highly desirable final resting place, and it quickly filled with those seeking eternal peace.

As the centuries wore on, the cemetery faced an ever-growing problem: there was simply no more space to accommodate the mounting number of burials. To address this issue, the decision was made to exhume the remains of thousands of individuals and move them into the ossuary beneath the Church of All Saints. In 1511, a half-blind monk was tasked with the unenviable job of exhuming and stacking the bones within the ossuary.

The true transformation of the Sedlec Ossuary began in 1870 when a woodcarver named Frantisek Rint was commissioned to artistically arrange the bones. Rint's work is a testament to his macabre creativity: he fashioned enormous chalices, a coat of arms for the Schwarzenberg family who had commissioned him, and a stunning chandelier that contains at least one of every bone found in the human body.

While the history of the Sedlec Ossuary is fascinating in its own right, it is the stories of the enigmatic entities and chilling legends that surround the "Bone Church" that truly capture the attention of those who venture within its walls.

Over the centuries, numerous accounts of strange occurrences and paranormal activity have been reported at the Sedlec Ossuary. From the faint sound of whispers and footsteps echoing through the chapel to the inexplicable sensation of being watched, there is no shortage of eerie tales that lend themselves to the belief that the ossuary is haunted by entities that defy explanation.

One such account comes from a historian who visited the ossuary in the early 1900s. As he wandered through the bone-laden chapel, he felt a sudden chill in the air, and the hairs on the back of his neck stood on end. He turned to find himself face-to-face with a spectral figure, dressed in tattered clothing and appearing as if it were made of mist. The figure seemed to be attempting to communicate with the historian, its mouth moving soundlessly as it reached out towards him. Overwhelmed by fear, the historian fled the ossuary, but the encounter remained etched in his memory for the rest of his life.

Another tale involves a group of paranormal investigators who visited the Sedlec Ossuary in the hopes of capturing evidence of the supernatural. As they set up their equipment, the group began to feel an overwhelming sense of unease, as though they were not alone. Throughout the night, the investigators experienced unexplained cold spots, fleeting shadows, and the distinct feeling of being touched by unseen hands. When they reviewed their audio recordings, they discovered what sounded like hushed voices and distant footsteps that had not been audible during their investigation. The unsettling findings further fueled the belief that the Sedlec Ossuary was indeed haunted by otherworldly entities.

Perhaps one of the most disturbing stories associated with the "Bone Church" is that of a young couple who ventured inside the ossuary after hours, seeking a thrilling experience in the darkness. As they made their way through the bone-filled chambers, they began to hear what sounded like faint weeping. Curiosity and fear mingling, they followed the sound to a corner of the ossuary where they encountered a ghostly figure, its transparent form seemingly wracked with sorrow as it knelt among the bones.

The couple, unable to tear their eyes away from the apparition, watched in horror as the figure slowly turned to face them. Its eyes, devoid of any light, seemed to pierce their very souls as it let out a heart-wrenching wail. The sound reverberated through the ossuary, and the couple fled in terror, forever haunted by the memory of their encounter with the grieving spectre.

The enigmatic entities that are said to reside within the walls of the Sedlec Ossuary have captured the attention of countless visitors over the years, and many have found themselves inexplicably drawn to the "Bone Church" in search of answers. Some believe that the spirits of those whose bones adorn the ossuary are trapped within its confines, unable to find peace in the afterlife. Others theorise that the ossuary's macabre atmosphere serves as a magnet for restless spirits, who are drawn to the energy that permeates the air within the chapel.

Regardless of the reasons behind the alleged hauntings, the chilling legends and paranormal activity associated with the Sedlec Ossuary continue to fascinate those who dare to delve into the eerie world of the "Bone Church." As they wander through the maze of artfully arranged bones, visitors are left with an indelible sense of unease, as though the very air within the ossuary is thick with the presence of unseen entities. Whether the result of overactive imaginations or genuine encounters with the supernatural, the stories that surround the Sedlec Ossuary have become an integral part of its dark and mysterious allure.

In the end, the enigmatic entities of the Sedlec Ossuary continue to confound and intrigue those who seek to unravel the mysteries of the "Bone Church." The chilling legends that surround this macabre site serve as a testament to the enduring fascination with the unknown, and the tales of ghostly encounters and inexplicable phenomena have become an inextricable part of the ossuary's history. As visitors continue to flock to the Sedlec Ossuary in search of answers, the chapel's bone-filled chambers stand as a haunting reminder of the thin line that separates life from death, and the power of the human imagination to conjure the most chilling of tales.

The enigmatic entities of the Sedlec Ossuary invite us to delve deeper into the chilling legends that surround this unique and haunting site, and to consider the stories that have been passed down through the generations. As we explore the mysteries of the "Bone Church," we are left with an unsettling sense of the unknown, and the knowledge that sometimes, the most intriguing stories lie hidden in the shadows of our world's most sacred places.

The Haunted Halls of St. Michan's Church

Established in 1095, St. Michan's Church, one of the oldest churches in Dublin, has seen centuries of prayers, worship, and even macabre fascination. Constructed on the site of an early Viking chapel, the church has been rebuilt and restored throughout its long history, with the current structure dating back to the late 17th century. The simple exterior of the church, situated in the heart of Dublin's north inner city, belies the eerie secrets that lie beneath it. The true source of St. Michan's chilling allure is hidden below the church's stone floors, where the air is cool and the shadows cling to the walls, in the mysterious crypts that hold mummified remains.

The crypts of St. Michan's Church are as old as the church itself, constructed in the 11th century to serve as a final resting place for the remains of the city's elite. Built of limestone, the crypts provide a naturally cool and dry environment that has, over the centuries, preserved the bodies interred within. These crypts have drawn curious visitors and fascinated scholars for generations, but it is the reports of supernatural activity and eerie encounters that have truly solidified the church's reputation as a haunted site.

The mummies within St. Michan's crypts are the primary source of fascination for visitors, drawing people from around the world to witness their grim visages. The origins of the mummies are as diverse as they are intriguing. Some of the most well-known occupants of the crypts include the Sheares brothers, Henry and John, who were executed in 1798 for their role in the Irish Rebellion, and the remains of the highly respected mathematician and Archbishop of Dublin, Narcissus Marsh, interred in 1713.

As visitors descend into the crypts, the air grows colder, and the atmosphere becomes heavier. The mysterious mummies, with their skin stretched tight over their bony frames, lie within open caskets, gazing up at the living with empty eye sockets. It is said that the mummies can be felt watching visitors, as though their spirits remain trapped within their desiccated bodies, keeping a silent vigil over the crypts they have called home for centuries.

Though the mummies themselves are a source of fascination and unease, it is the reports of strange occurrences within the crypts that have truly earned St. Michan's its reputation as a haunted site. Visitors have reported feeling inexplicable cold spots and sudden gusts of air, despite the crypts being closed off from the outside environment. The sounds of faint whispers have been heard, echoing through the narrow passageways, and the sensation of unseen presences has left many feeling as though they are not alone among the long-dead inhabitants of the crypts.

One such account of a chilling encounter within St. Michan's crypts comes from a group of tourists who had ventured beneath the church to explore the hidden vaults. As they made their way through the dimly lit passageways, they were suddenly overcome by an overwhelming sense of dread, as though they were being watched from the shadows. The group quickly became disoriented, losing track of both time and their bearings within the crypts. As they attempted to retrace their steps, they heard the sound of footsteps behind them, the heavy thuds echoing through the narrow corridors. Despite their fear, the group turned to confront the source of the noise, only to find the passageway empty and the footsteps ceasing as suddenly as they had begun.

In another account, a local historian was conducting research within the crypts, attempting to piece together the stories and histories of those interred within. As he worked, he began to feel a sudden chill in the air, a coldness that seemed to emanate from one of the open caskets. The historian, attempting to dismiss his unease as a trick of his mind, continued his work. However, the sensation persisted, eventually accompanied by a feeling of being watched, as if the mummy within the casket was observing his every move. Unable to shake the sense of dread that had taken hold, the historian decided to leave the crypts, disturbed by the experience and unable to explain what had transpired.

These stories are just a few among many that have been shared by visitors and locals alike, each tale adding to the eerie reputation of St. Michan's Church and its enigmatic crypts. But it is not just the crypts that have given rise to tales of supernatural activity. Within the church itself, there have been reports of strange phenomena, such as ghostly figures seen wandering the aisles and unexplained sounds emanating from within the ancient walls.

One such story involves a couple who were visiting the church to attend a Sunday service. As they sat in the pews, listening to the sermon, they noticed a figure standing in the shadows near the back of the church. The figure, dressed in tattered robes, appeared to be watching the congregation, though no one else seemed to notice its presence. The couple, intrigued and unsettled, attempted to point out the figure to others around them, but as they did so, the figure seemed to simply vanish into thin air, leaving no trace of its presence.

Another account tells of a church caretaker who was locking up for the night, ensuring that all candles had been extinguished and that the church was secure. As he made his way through the darkened church, he heard the sound of organ music, faint but unmistakable. The caretaker, knowing that he was alone and that the organ should not be in use, cautiously approached the source of the music. As he neared the organ, the music grew louder and more distinct, yet there was no sign of anyone playing the instrument. The caretaker, unnerved by the inexplicable music, left the church, unable to explain what he had experienced.

These chilling encounters and eerie tales have cemented St. Michan's Church as a location of both historical and supernatural significance. The church and its crypts serve as a testament to the enduring fascination with the unknown, drawing those who seek to explore the mysteries that lie beneath the surface of our world. Whether through the enigmatic mummies that reside within the crypts or the ghostly phenomena that have been reported within the church itself, St. Michan's continues to captivate and intrigue those who dare to delve into its shadowy depths.

As we have explored the haunted halls of St. Michan's Church and the eerie vaults that lie beneath its ancient stones, we have borne witness to the powerful allure of the supernatural and the chilling encounters that have been experienced within its hallowed grounds. The stories of restless mummies and ghostly figures serve as a haunting reminder of the complex tapestry of history, emotion, and mystery that is woven into the very fabric of these sacred sites.

The haunted and the holy, intertwined through centuries of devotion, tragedy, and curiosity, continue to captivate the imaginations of those who seek to understand the world beyond our comprehension. It is within these ancient churches and sacred sites, where the echoes of the past reverberate through the air, that we are afforded a glimpse into the enigmatic realm of the supernatural, forever shrouded in shadows and whispered secrets.

The Grieving Bride of St. Olaf's Church

Tallinn, Estonia, a city steeped in history and architectural splendour, is home to a myriad of ancient structures that have stood the test of time. St. Olaf's Church, a towering gothic masterpiece, is one such structure that has witnessed the ebb and flow of human civilization throughout the centuries. With its soaring spire that once reached dizzying heights, St. Olaf's Church casts an imposing shadow over the city's skyline, inviting visitors to explore its rich past and uncover the secrets that lie within its hallowed walls.

The origins of St. Olaf's Church date back to the 12th century when it was first constructed as a Catholic church dedicated to King Olaf II of Norway, a patron saint of the country. The church has withstood numerous fires, wars, and invasions, yet it has endured, becoming a symbol of Tallinn's resilience and unwavering spirit. Over time, St. Olaf's has transitioned from a

Catholic to a Lutheran church, a reflection of Estonia's tumultuous religious history.

Within the ancient walls of St. Olaf's Church, a tragic love story has taken root, one that is said to have left an indelible mark on the spiritual fabric of the church itself. The tale speaks of a young woman, a bride-to-be, whose life was cut short on the eve of her wedding day. As legend has it, the bride, a beautiful and vibrant young woman named Liisa, was to marry her beloved fiancé, a dashing and promising young man named Jaan. However, fate had other plans for the star-crossed lovers.

In the days leading up to their wedding, an outbreak of disease swept through the city, claiming the lives of many, including Jaan. Devastated by her loss, Liisa, dressed in her wedding gown, entered St. Olaf's Church to pray for her beloved's soul. Overcome with grief, she fell to the ground, her lifeless body joining that of her fiancé in eternal rest.

Since that fateful day, numerous visitors to St. Olaf's Church have reported encountering a ghostly figure, believed to be the spirit of the grieving bride, Liisa. Clad in her ethereal wedding gown, she is said to wander the church's grounds and interior, searching for her lost love, Jaan.

The accounts of Liisa's ghostly apparitions are as varied as the individuals who have witnessed them. Some have reported seeing her translucent figure glide through the church's nave, her anguished expression conveying an unbearable sorrow. Others have heard the faint sound of weeping, echoing through the hallowed halls, a haunting reminder of the heartbreak that befell the ill-fated bride.

One particular encounter with the grieving bride's spirit stands out among the many tales. A group of tourists visiting the church one evening reported seeing a ghostly figure in the churchyard, bathed in the silvery light of the moon. They claimed that as they approached the figure, it suddenly vanished, leaving behind a palpable sense of sadness that seemed to linger in the air.

The heartrending tale of Liisa and Jaan is but one of many stories that permeate the storied history of St. Olaf's Church. The church, with its long and complex past, has borne witness to countless events that have shaped the lives of those who sought solace within its walls. As a result, it is not surprising that a tale as powerful and poignant as that of the grieving bride should leave an indelible mark on the spiritual landscape of the church.

In addition to the apparition of the grieving bride, St. Olaf's

Church has been the site of other unexplained phenomena, further adding to its mystique as a place where the extraordinary and inexplicable converge. Visitors have reported strange, disembodied voices and unexplained sounds emanating from within the church, with no discernible source. Others have felt inexplicable cold spots or a sudden, overwhelming sense of unease as they traversed the ancient building.

Historians and paranormal enthusiasts alike have sought to uncover the truth behind these mysterious occurrences, attempting to unravel the threads of history that have intertwined to create the tapestry of the haunted church. Some believe that the church's long and storied past, punctuated by periods of strife, violence, and upheaval, has left a lasting imprint on its spiritual energy, giving rise to the supernatural phenomena experienced by those who visit its hallowed grounds.

Others attribute the ghostly encounters and unexplained occurrences to the power of the collective imagination, suggesting that the tales of St. Olaf's haunting have become so ingrained in the city's folklore that they have taken on a life of their own, manifesting as spectral visions and eerie sensations. Regardless of the explanation, the stories surrounding St. Olaf's

Church serve as a testament to the enduring power of love and loss, transcending the boundaries of time and space to touch the hearts and minds of those who hear them.

The haunting beauty of St. Olaf's Church, with its gothic architecture and storied past, continues to captivate visitors from around the world. Its towering spire, which once served as a beacon for sailors navigating the treacherous waters of the Baltic Sea, now stands as a testament to the resilience and indomitable spirit of the people of Tallinn.

As visitors explore the ancient halls and hallowed grounds of St. Olaf's Church, they cannot help but be moved by the tragic tale of the grieving bride and her lost love. The ghostly apparitions and unexplained phenomena that haunt the church serve as a poignant reminder of the profound emotions that bind us to this world and the mysteries that lie just beyond the reach of our understanding.

In the hallowed halls of St. Olaf's Church, where the echoes of history reverberate through time, a grieving bride continues her eternal search for the love she lost, her spectral presence a haunting testament to the power of love, even in the face of the greatest adversity.

As we continue our exploration of haunted churches and sacred sites, we carry with us the stories of those who came before us, their lives forever intertwined with the ancient structures that have borne witness to their triumphs, their sorrows, and their indomitable spirit. In the case of St. Olaf's Church and the grieving bride, we are reminded of the enduring human capacity for love and devotion, a force that transcends the boundaries of life and death, drawing us ever closer to the mysteries that lie at the heart of our existence.

From the ghostly apparitions that haunt the hallowed grounds of St. Olaf's Church to the unexplained phenomena that defy explanation, the tale of the grieving bride serves as a powerful reminder of the human capacity for love, loss, and the enduring mystery of the unknown. As we delve deeper into the world of haunted churches and sacred sites, we cannot help but wonder what other secrets lie hidden within their ancient walls, waiting to be discovered by those brave enough to venture into the shadows.

The Sinister Shadows of St. Bartholomew-the-Great

The streets of London, one of the most historically rich and culturally diverse cities in the world, are home to a vast array of architectural wonders that span centuries. Amidst the hustle and bustle of modern life, the city's ancient structures stand as silent witnesses to the passage of time. Among these storied edifices, one particular sacred site has captured the imagination of those who seek to unravel the mysteries of the supernatural world: St. Bartholomew-the-Great.

The priory, founded by Rahere, a courtier to King Henry I, in 1123, was originally an Augustinian monastery. Rahere's vision for the church came to him after a life-changing pilgrimage to Rome, during which he fell gravely ill. He experienced a miraculous vision of St. Bartholomew, who instructed him to establish a church and hospital in London. Upon his return to England, Rahere fulfilled this divine command, and St.

Bartholomew-the-Great was born.

As the oldest surviving church in London, St. Bartholomew-the-Great has borne witness to some of the most significant events in British history. The church survived the dissolution of the monasteries in the 16th century, albeit significantly reduced in size, and even managed to endure the Great Fire of London in 1666. The tumultuous history of this ancient site has left a lasting impression on the very fabric of the building, and it is perhaps unsurprising that tales of malevolent entities and unexplained phenomena have become entwined with the priory's storied past.

One such tale is that of the sinister shadow that stalks the church's Lady Chapel. This shadowy figure, often described as a monk-like apparition cloaked in darkness, has been seen by many who have dared to venture within the chapel's hallowed walls. Some believe that the shadowy figure is the spirit of a malevolent monk who, in life, succumbed to the darker impulses of his nature, committing heinous acts that left an indelible mark on the church's history.

The haunting of the Lady Chapel is not the only supernatural occurrence to have been reported at St. Bartholomew-the-Great.

In the church's crypt, visitors have experienced a palpable sense of unease, as if the weight of centuries of sorrow and suffering has left an imprint on the very air itself. Some have reported feeling an unseen presence, a spectral force that seems to emanate from the dark corners of the crypt, leaving those who enter with a feeling of dread that is difficult to shake.

These unexplained phenomena have been the subject of much debate and investigation over the years. One particularly chilling account comes from a local historian, who, in the late 19th century, was conducting research on the priory's past. As the historian worked late into the night within the crypt, he began to hear faint, disembodied whispers that seemed to emanate from the darkness itself. As the whispers grew louder, he felt an inexplicable sense of terror overcome him, and fled the crypt in a state of panic, vowing never to return.

Another eyewitness account comes from a visitor to the church in the early 20th century. While exploring the Lady Chapel, the visitor was overcome by an overwhelming sense of dread, as if a malevolent force was watching her from the shadows. As she turned to leave, she caught a glimpse of a dark, hooded figure standing in the corner of the chapel, its eyes fixed on her with an intensity that chilled her to the bone.

The tales of sinister shadows and unexplained phenomena within St. Bartholomew-the-Great have persisted into the modern era, with numerous visitors recounting their own chilling encounters within the ancient priory. One such account comes from a couple who, in the early 2000s, attended a candlelit evening service at the church. As they sat in the flickering candlelight, they both became aware of a distinct feeling of unease. They later reported that they felt as if they were being watched by a malevolent presence, its gaze fixed upon them from the shadows.

Following the service, the couple decided to explore the crypt, despite the lingering sense of unease that had plagued them throughout the evening. As they descended the narrow staircase into the darkness below, they were overcome by a sudden, bone-chilling drop in temperature. The air in the crypt seemed thick with an oppressive atmosphere, as if centuries of pain and suffering had seeped into the very walls.

As they made their way through the crypt, the couple noticed that the feeling of being watched had intensified, and they could not shake the sensation that they were not alone. Upon leaving the crypt, they later reported feeling a palpable sense of relief, as if a malevolent force had been left behind in the depths of the ancient priory.

Although the stories of hauntings and unexplained phenomena within St. Bartholomew-the-Great have never been definitively proven, the weight of centuries of history and the enduring tales of sinister shadows and malevolent entities continue to draw curious souls to this ancient London priory. As visitors explore the hallowed halls and hidden corners of this venerable building, they cannot help but wonder if the dark past of St. Bartholomew-the-Great has given rise to the unexplained phenomena and chilling encounters that continue to haunt its storied halls.

In the heart of London, St. Bartholomew-the-Great stands as a testament to the enduring power of the human spirit, and the mysteries that lie just beyond our comprehension. As the city continues to evolve and grow around it, the ancient priory remains a beacon of history and a reminder of the countless souls who have sought solace within its walls.

The tales of malevolent entities and unexplained phenomena that surround St. Bartholomew-the-Great serve as a chilling counterpoint to the tranquillity that the church offers its visitors. As each new generation seeks to unravel the mysteries that lie within the priory's ancient walls, the stories of the sinister shadows and the restless spirits that are said to dwell there continue to capture the imagination of those who dare to explore the darker corners of history.

In the end, the truth behind the hauntings of St. Bartholomew-the-Great may forever remain shrouded in mystery. But one thing is certain: the tales of the supernatural that have become entwined with the history of this ancient London priory will continue to captivate the hearts and minds of those who seek to understand the mysteries of the world beyond our understanding. And as the shadows lengthen and the darkness falls, the malevolent entities and unexplained phenomena that are said to haunt St. Bartholomew-the-Great will continue to draw the curious and the brave, daring them to venture within and uncover the secrets that lie within the hallowed halls of this mediaeval London priory.

The Poltergeists of St. Andrew's on the Red

In the vast expanse of the Canadian wilderness, shrouded in the mists of time and myth, lies the historic St. Andrew's on the Red. This ancient church, situated on the banks of the Red River in the province of Manitoba, has long been a beacon of spirituality and a sacred haven for those seeking solace and communion with the divine. Yet, beneath the serene facade of this stately edifice, a darker presence lingers, one that has given rise to chilling tales of ghostly encounters and inexplicable happenings that continue to echo through the centuries.

Constructed in the early 19th century, St. Andrew's on the Red is an enduring testament to the indomitable spirit of the early settlers who braved the harsh Canadian wilderness to forge a new life in this untamed land. The church's imposing stone structure, with its Gothic Revival-style architecture and soaring spire, stands as a proud symbol of the faith and resilience of the community that it has served for nearly two centuries. Yet, as with any edifice of such age and history, St. Andrew's on the Red has borne witness to countless human dramas, tragedies, and triumphs, and it is within the hallowed halls of this storied church that the spirits of the past are said to still linger, their presence manifesting in chilling encounters and mysterious happenings that defy rational explanation.

The history of St. Andrew's on the Red is a rich tapestry of human experience, woven from the lives and stories of the generations who have sought refuge within its walls. Built in 1844 by the Rev. William Cockran, an Anglican missionary who was instrumental in establishing the Church of England in the Red River Settlement, the church has served as a vital centre of community life and spiritual nourishment for the diverse population of settlers, traders, and indigenous peoples who called this rugged landscape home.

As the years passed and the community grew, the church became a repository of memories and experiences, each leaving its indelible mark on the fabric of the building. Within its walls, generations of families have celebrated the joy of baptisms and weddings, and mourned the loss of loved ones in funerals and memorials. The echoes of laughter, tears, and whispered prayers have resonated through the church, imbuing the very stones with the essence of the human spirit.

It is perhaps no wonder, then, that the history of St. Andrew's on the Red has become entwined with tales of the supernatural and the unexplained. The church, with its long-standing connection to the lives and emotions of those who have sought solace within its walls, seems to have become a conduit for the spiritual energy that flows between our world and the realm of the unknown. Over the years, numerous visitors and parishioners have reported chilling encounters and eerie happenings within the church, from disembodied voices and ghostly apparitions to inexplicable poltergeist activity that has left even the most hardened sceptics questioning their understanding of the world.

One of the most enduring tales of paranormal activity at St. Andrew's on the Red concerns a series of unexplained events that took place in the late 19th century, during the tenure of the Rev. Henry George. A deeply spiritual man, Rev. George was well-respected in the community for his dedication to his parishioners and his unwavering faith in the power of the divine. Yet, despite his steadfast devotion, Rev. George would find himself at the centre of a chilling mystery that would challenge the very foundations of his belief.

The events in question began on a cold winter's night, when Rev. George was alone in the church, preparing for the following day's service. As he moved through the dimly lit sanctuary, he was suddenly struck by a sensation of overwhelming unease, as if an unseen presence was watching him from the shadows. Shaking off the feeling as a product of his own imagination, Rev. George continued with his preparations, only to be startled by a loud crash emanating from the back of the church.

Upon investigating, the reverend found that several heavy hymnals had been inexplicably hurled from their shelves, scattering across the floor as if propelled by an unseen force. Disturbed by the event, Rev. George quickly finished his work and left the church, his mind filled with troubling questions about the nature of the force that had made its presence known.

In the days and weeks that followed, the mysterious happenings within the church continued, as Rev. George and his parishioners experienced a series of inexplicable events that seemed to defy all rational explanation. Objects would be moved or thrown by an invisible hand, doors would slam shut without warning, and strange sounds and whispers would fill the air, seemingly emanating from the very walls of the church itself.

As the tales of the strange occurrences at St. Andrew's on the Red spread throughout the community, many began to speculate about the possible source of the supernatural activity. Some believed that the church was haunted by the restless spirits of the deceased who had been laid to rest in the nearby cemetery, while others suggested that the ancient site upon which the church was built was home to powerful energies that could manifest in mysterious and sometimes terrifying ways.

Over the years, numerous eyewitnesses have come forward with their own stories of eerie encounters and chilling experiences at St. Andrew's on the Red. One such account comes from a local woman named Sarah, who visited the church with her family in the 1970s. As they explored the historic building, Sarah was suddenly overcome by an intense feeling of dread, as if the air around her had become heavy and oppressive. Unable to shake the sensation, she left the church, only to later learn that her ancestors had a tragic connection to the very spot where she had experienced her unsettling encounter.

Another tale comes from a man named Tom, who was attending a late-night vigil at the church when he witnessed a series of bizarre events that would stay with him for the rest of his life. As the congregation prayed in silence, the candles that illuminated the sanctuary began to flicker and dim, as if an unseen presence was moving through the room. Suddenly, the air was filled with the sound of disembodied footsteps, which seemed to echo through the church, growing louder and more insistent with each passing moment. The congregation, now gripped with fear, hurriedly left the church, their prayers giving way to whispered speculation about the nature of the entity that had made its presence known.

The stories of ghostly happenings and poltergeist activity at St. Andrew's on the Red have continued to captivate the imaginations of locals and visitors alike, drawing curious souls from around the world to this remote corner of Manitoba in search of answers to the mysteries that lie within its walls. Many have sought to explain the phenomena through the lens of science or psychology, attributing the eerie occurrences to natural forces or the power of suggestion. Yet, despite the myriad theories and conjectures, the truth behind the haunting of St. Andrew's on the Red remains an enigma, as elusive and inscrutable as the spirits that are said to dwell within its hallowed halls.

As we reflect on the chilling tales and mysterious happenings that surround this historic church, it is evident that St. Andrew's on the Red offers a unique window into the world of the supernatural and the unexplained.

The Watchful Spirits of St. Augustine's Monastery

The ancient St. Augustine's Monastery, situated in Erfurt, Germany, is a breathtaking example of Gothic architecture. The monastery was established in the 13th century and played a significant role in the religious and intellectual life of the region for centuries. Home to the famous theologian and reformer Martin Luther, who lived within its walls as an Augustinian monk, St. Augustine's Monastery stands as a testament to the enduring influence of faith and scholarship. However, as captivating as its rich history and architectural beauty may be, the monastery is also known for its eerie presence and tales of paranormal activity that continue to intrigue visitors from all over the world.

The history of St. Augustine's Monastery stretches back to its founding in 1277 when the Augustinian Hermits established a community within the city of Erfurt. As the community flourished, the monastery expanded its physical presence and its influence in the region, becoming a centre of learning and religious study. In the early 16th century, the monastery was at the heart of the intellectual and religious ferment that would give rise to the Protestant Reformation, as Martin Luther joined its ranks as a novice monk in 1505. The time Luther spent within the walls of St. Augustine's Monastery would have a profound impact on his life and work, setting the stage for the seismic religious upheaval that would reshape Europe and the Christian world.

Yet, beyond its storied history and impressive architecture, St. Augustine's Monastery is also the backdrop for a multitude of chilling tales and inexplicable occurrences that seem to defy rational explanation. For centuries, visitors have reported encountering an eerie presence within the monastery's hallowed halls, as if the spirits of the past continue to watch over their sacred home. From ghostly apparitions to unexplained sounds and movements, the monastery has become a focal point for those seeking to delve into the mysteries of the paranormal.

One of the most enduring tales of the paranormal activity at St. Augustine's Monastery centres around the apparition of a hooded monk, believed by some to be the spirit of Martin Luther himself. The figure has been seen roaming the monastery's corridors and grounds, often vanishing as suddenly as it appears. Some witnesses have described the apparition as benevolent, even comforting, while others have been left with a sense of unease and trepidation after their encounters with the spectral monk.

In addition to the apparition of the hooded monk, visitors to St. Augustine's Monastery have reported a variety of other unexplained phenomena, such as disembodied voices and footsteps echoing through the empty halls. Many have claimed to hear the faint sound of Gregorian chants drifting through the air, as if the long-deceased monks continue to perform their sacred rites. Others have reported feeling a sudden chill or a gentle touch, as if an unseen presence is attempting to make its presence known.

One particularly chilling account comes from a group of tourists who visited the monastery in the late 20th century. As they explored the ancient structure, they were startled to hear the sound of a door slamming shut, followed by the distinct sound of footsteps approaching. Despite their frantic search, the group could find no source for the mysterious sounds, leaving them to wonder if they had stumbled upon the restless spirits that are said to inhabit the monastery's hallowed halls.

Another tale comes from a local historian, who was conducting research within the monastery's extensive library. As he delved into the ancient texts, he became aware of a strange sensation, as if he were being watched by unseen eyes. Glancing up from his work, he caught sight of a spectral figure standing at the far end of the room, dressed in the traditional garb of an Augustinian monk. The figure seemed to shimmer and fade, like a mirage, before disappearing completely. The historian, shaken by the encounter, could not explain the strange vision he had witnessed but felt certain that he had come face-to-face with one of the watchful spirits said to roam St. Augustine's Monastery.

The various accounts of paranormal activity at St. Augustine's Monastery have led many to speculate on the reasons behind the seemingly supernatural occurrences. Some attribute the hauntings to the monastery's long and storied history, suggesting that the spirits of monks and scholars who once called the abbey home may be reluctant to leave their sacred sanctuary. Others believe that the monastery may serve as a portal to another realm, allowing the spirits of the departed to return and make their presence known.

Regardless of the cause, the tales of paranormal activity at St. Augustine's Monastery have made it a popular destination for both the curious and the courageous. Visitors from around the world continue to flock to the ancient abbey, drawn by its captivating history, architectural beauty, and the promise of an encounter with the unknown.

As one explores the hallowed halls and sacred grounds of St. Augustine's Monastery, it is impossible not to feel the weight of history and the echoes of the past that permeate the very air. The monastery stands as a testament to the power of faith, the pursuit of knowledge, and the indomitable human spirit. Yet, within its walls, there also exists a world of mystery, where the inexplicable and the supernatural coexist with the rational and the mundane.

The watchful spirits of St. Augustine's Monastery serve as a reminder of the complex tapestry of human existence, weaving together the material and the immaterial, the sacred and the profane. As we delve into the enigmatic tales and chilling encounters that have come to define this ancient abbey, we are left to ponder the nature of the world that lies just beyond our grasp, a world of shadows and whispers that seems to defy our attempts to comprehend its mysteries.

In the end, the stories of St. Augustine's Monastery, like those of the other haunted churches and sacred sites we have explored, offer a unique window into the unseen realms that coexist with our own. They challenge us to confront the limits of our understanding and to consider the possibility that there may be more to our world than meets the eye. It is this sense of mystery and wonder that continues to draw us to these ancient sanctuaries, as we seek to unravel the secrets that lie within their hallowed halls.

The Phantom Friars of Greyfriars Kirkyard

Greyfriars Kirkyard, located in the heart of Edinburgh, Scotland, is a burial ground steeped in history and shrouded in a cloak of chilling legends. Established in the 16th century, the cemetery has served as the final resting place for a multitude of notable figures, including poets, politicians, and philosophers. Over the centuries, the atmospheric graveyard has become infamous for the eerie encounters and haunting tales that surround it. From the shadowy corners of the ancient burial ground to the ghostly apparitions that are said to roam its pathways, Greyfriars Kirkyard has earned its place among the most haunted churches and sacred sites in the world.

The history of Greyfriars Kirkyard can be traced back to the early years of the 16th century when it was founded on the grounds of a Franciscan friary. The friary, home to an order of monks known as the Greyfriars, derived its name from the grey habits worn by its inhabitants. Following the Scottish Reformation in the mid-16th century, the friary fell into disrepair and was eventually abandoned. However, its hallowed grounds continued to serve as a burial site, with the first interment taking place in 1562.

Over the years, Greyfriars Kirkyard has been the scene of numerous historic events, many of which have left a lasting impact on the cemetery's ethereal atmosphere. One such event was the signing of the National Covenant in 1638, a declaration of religious and civil liberties that led to a series of armed conflicts known as the Wars of the Three Kingdoms. The memory of this turbulent period in Scottish history is preserved within the walls of the Covenanters' Prison, a section of the cemetery where hundreds of men were held captive under inhumane conditions. The suffering and despair that marked this dark chapter in Greyfriars Kirkyard's history have become indelibly etched in its very fabric, adding to the sense of unease that pervades the burial ground.

In addition to its historic significance, Greyfriars Kirkyard has gained a reputation for the seemingly supernatural occurrences that have been reported within its boundaries. Visitors to the cemetery have recounted a host of eerie experiences, from sudden drops in temperature to the inexplicable sensation of being watched by unseen eyes. Amidst the moss-covered tombstones and ancient mausoleums, a sense of foreboding hangs in the air, as though the spirits of the departed are unwilling to relinquish their grip on the mortal realm.

Central to the legends of Greyfriars Kirkyard are the phantom friars, spectral figures said to roam the cemetery's labyrinthine pathways. Clad in the distinctive grey habits of their order, these ghostly apparitions have been sighted by numerous witnesses, their silent presence an eerie reminder of the cemetery's monastic origins. Although their motives remain unclear, many speculate that the phantom friars may be bound to the site of their former home, their spirits tethered to the burial ground by the force of their religious convictions.

One of the most famous spectral residents of Greyfriars Kirkyard is the malevolent spirit known as the Mackenzie Poltergeist. This sinister entity is said to be the restless spirit of Sir George Mackenzie, a 17th-century lawyer and Lord Advocate who was responsible for the persecution of the Covenanters. It is believed that the malevolent spirit was unleashed in 1998 when a homeless man seeking shelter unwittingly disturbed Mackenzie's tomb. Since then, visitors to the cemetery have reported being violently attacked by an unseen force, suffering scratches, bruises, and even burns after encountering the malevolent spirit. The chilling tales of the Mackenzie Poltergeist have only served to bolster Greyfriars Kirkyard's reputation as a hotbed of paranormal activity.

In contrast to the malevolent presence of the Mackenzie Poltergeist, other spirits that are said to inhabit Greyfriars Kirkyard are believed to be more benign in nature. Among them is the ghostly figure of a young girl known as Annie, who is said to have died from the plague in the 17th century. Visitors to the cemetery have reported encountering the spirit of Annie near the tomb of Sir George Mackenzie, where she is often seen in the company of the cemetery's other spectral residents. In a heartwarming display of empathy, many visitors to Greyfriars Kirkyard have left tokens and toys at the site of Annie's grave, in the hope of providing comfort to the spirit of the young girl who was taken from the world too soon.

As one delves deeper into the haunted history of Greyfriars Kirkyard, it becomes apparent that the cemetery's spectral inhabitants have transcended the boundaries of time and space to leave an indelible mark on the living world. Eyewitness accounts of encounters with these ethereal entities have proliferated over the years, with many visitors to the cemetery sharing their spine-chilling experiences in hushed whispers and anxious tones.

One such account comes from a woman named Mary, who visited Greyfriars Kirkyard on a guided tour in the early 2000s. As she walked through the cemetery's shadowy pathways, Mary reported feeling an icy chill in the air, accompanied by an overwhelming sense of dread. As she turned a corner, she caught sight of a hooded figure clad in grey robes, standing motionless among the tombstones. The spectral figure appeared to be observing her from a distance, its face obscured by the shadows. Although the encounter lasted for only a few seconds, the image of the phantom friar has remained seared into Mary's memory, a haunting reminder of her brush with the unknown.

Another eyewitness account comes from a man named James, who visited Greyfriars Kirkyard with a group of friends in the late 1990s. As they wandered through the cemetery, James noticed that one of his companions, a young woman named Sarah, had become increasingly agitated. When questioned, Sarah confessed that she felt as though she was being watched by unseen eyes. Moments later, she let out a piercing scream, claiming that she had seen a hooded figure emerge from the shadows and approach her. The figure, which Sarah described as a ghostly monk dressed in tattered grey robes, appeared to be attempting to communicate with her, its outstretched hand reaching toward her face. The group fled the cemetery in terror, their hearts pounding as they sought to escape the eerie presence that seemed to pursue them through the darkness.

The haunting tales and spine-chilling encounters that have become synonymous with Greyfriars Kirkyard offer a window into a world where the boundaries between the living and the dead appear to be permeable. As the sun sets and the shadows lengthen, the cemetery's spectral inhabitants emerge from the darkness, their ghostly forms a chilling testament to the enduring power of history and the mysteries that lie just beyond our understanding.

As we draw our exploration of Greyfriars Kirkyard to a close, it is evident that the phantom friars and other spectral figures that are said to wander the cemetery's hallowed grounds have left an indelible mark on the collective consciousness.

The Crying Madonna of Syracuse

In the sun-kissed coastal city of Syracuse, on the southeastern shores of Sicily, there is a sacred shrine that has captured the hearts and imaginations of both believers and non-believers alike. For centuries, the Church of Santa Lucia al Sepolcro has been a focal point for devotees and curious visitors seeking solace, redemption, and a glimpse into the world of the divine. At the heart of this storied sanctuary lies a miraculous statue of the Madonna, whose tearful countenance has been the subject of awe, intrigue, and countless whispered tales. In this chapter, we delve into the enigmatic history of the Crying Madonna of Syracuse, unearthing the stories of supernatural events that have left an indelible mark on this sacred Italian shrine.

The history of the Church of Santa Lucia al Sepolcro is inextricably intertwined with the life of Saint Lucy, the patron saint of Syracuse. Born in the late third century AD, Saint Lucy is renowned for her unwavering faith and commitment to Christian ideals. Legend has it that during her short life, she took a vow of virginity and devoted herself to the service of the poor and needy. Her steadfast beliefs, however, led to her tragic demise at the hands of the Roman authorities during the Diocletianic Persecution.

Saint Lucy's life and martyrdom have left a lasting impression on the people of Syracuse, who hold her in high esteem as a symbol of courage, faith, and devotion. It is within the walls of the Church of Santa Lucia al Sepolcro that her story lives on, preserved for posterity in the form of exquisite frescoes, mosaics, and sculptures that adorn the sacred space. The church itself, a stunning example of Baroque architecture, was constructed over the ruins of an ancient temple dedicated to the Roman goddess Diana. It is this unique blend of the old and the new, the pagan and the Christian, that lends the Church of Santa Lucia al Sepolcro its air of mystique.

At the heart of the church's enigmatic history is the miraculous statue of the Madonna, known as the Crying Madonna of Syracuse. The life-size sculpture, carved from pure white marble, is a masterpiece of artistic expression and spiritual devotion. Its creator, the renowned Italian sculptor Antonello Gagini, was a man of prodigious talent and unwavering faith, who sought to bring the divine to life through his creations.

The story of the Crying Madonna of Syracuse dates back to the early 16th century when Gagini was commissioned by the church to create a statue in honour of the Virgin Mary. Working tirelessly, Gagini poured his heart and soul into the project, imbuing the statue with a sense of piety, grace, and spiritual depth. The end result was a magnificent work of art that soon became the focal point of the church, drawing the faithful from far and wide to pay homage to the Mother of Christ.

It was not long after the statue's completion that rumours began to circulate about a series of inexplicable events surrounding the Crying Madonna of Syracuse. Visitors to the church reported witnessing tears streaming down the statue's face, as if the Virgin Mary herself was mourning the pain and suffering of the world. The phenomenon, which seemed to defy all rational explanation, soon gained notoriety, drawing curious onlookers and devout believers alike.

The tears of the Crying Madonna of Syracuse were not the only supernatural events associated with the statue. Over the years, numerous eyewitness accounts have emerged detailing miraculous healings and other divine interventions attributed to the Madonna. Stories abound of blind men and women regaining their sight, the lame walking, and the sick being cured of their ailments after praying before the statue. These accounts have cemented the Crying Madonna of Syracuse's reputation as a beacon of hope and a symbol of divine grace, attracting pilgrims and devotees from all corners of the globe.

One particularly poignant account comes from a local fisherman named Giuseppe, who claimed to have been miraculously healed of his chronic back pain after praying before the Crying Madonna of Syracuse. According to Giuseppe, he had been plagued by excruciating pain for years, which rendered him unable to work and support his family. Desperate for relief, he sought solace at the church and prayed fervently before the statue. To his amazement, the pain vanished almost instantaneously, and he was able to resume his work as a fisherman, free from the debilitating agony that had once defined his life.

Another remarkable story involves a young girl named Maria, who was said to have been cured of a life-threatening illness after her mother prayed to the Crying Madonna of Syracuse for her recovery. Maria had been bedridden for months, with doctors unable to provide a diagnosis or any hope of improvement. In a final act of desperation, her mother sought the intervention of the Madonna, placing her faith in the divine. Miraculously, Maria's condition began to improve, and she eventually made a full recovery, much to the astonishment of her doctors and family members.

In addition to the miraculous healings, there have been reports of other supernatural events surrounding the Crying Madonna of Syracuse. Some visitors to the church have described a palpable energy emanating from the statue, as if the very air around it was charged with a divine presence. Others have reported experiencing an overwhelming sense of peace and serenity while in the presence of the statue, as if the Madonna's tears held the power to cleanse and purify the soul.

Sceptics, of course, have sought alternative explanations for the phenomena associated with the Crying Madonna of Syracuse. Some have posited that the tears are nothing more than a natural occurrence, the result of condensation forming on the cold marble surface of the statue. Others have suggested that the miraculous healings can be attributed to the power of suggestion, with the fervent belief of the afflicted individuals playing a crucial role in their recovery.

Despite these alternative explanations, the faithful remain undeterred in their conviction that the Crying Madonna of Syracuse is a genuine manifestation of the divine. For them, the statue is a testament to the power of faith and the enduring presence of the divine in our world, offering hope and solace to those who seek it.

As we delve into the enigmatic history of the Crying Madonna of Syracuse, it becomes clear that the true significance of this sacred statue lies not in the debates surrounding its miraculous nature but in the stories of the countless individuals who have found hope, healing, and redemption in its presence. These stories, passed down through generations, speak to the profound impact that the Crying Madonna of Syracuse has had on the lives of those who have encountered it. In a world filled with pain and suffering, the statue stands as a symbol of hope and a reminder that, in the face of adversity, faith can provide a guiding light.

In the hallowed halls of the Church of Santa Lucia al Sepolcro, the Crying Madonna of Syracuse continues to draw the faithful and the curious, offering a glimpse into a world where the divine and the human intersect. As we leave the sun-drenched shores of Sicily behind, we carry with us the stories of the miraculous weeping statue and the supernatural events that have unfolded within the walls of this sacred Italian shrine.

The Mysterious Apparitions of St. Mark's Basilica

In the heart of Venice, Italy, the imposing edifice of St. Mark's Basilica rises majestically above the bustling city. A symbol of the city's rich history and artistic heritage, this awe-inspiring cathedral has been a site of worship, pilgrimage, and architectural marvel for centuries. Yet, amidst the grandeur of its gilded mosaics and soaring domes, the Basilica conceals a darker side – a realm of mysterious apparitions and otherworldly phenomena that has long intrigued both believers and sceptics alike.

The history of St. Mark's Basilica dates back to the 9th century when it was first constructed as a private chapel to house the relics of St. Mark, the patron saint of Venice. Over time, the church evolved into an architectural masterpiece, with Byzantine, Romanesque, and Gothic influences blending harmoniously to create a unique and captivating structure. The

Basilica's interior is adorned with intricate mosaics, ornate marble carvings, and precious artefacts that attest to the wealth and power of the Venetian Republic in its heyday.

While the grandiosity and opulence of St. Mark's Basilica are undeniable, it is the enigmatic tales of apparitions and supernatural occurrences that have shrouded the cathedral in a veil of mystery. Throughout its storied history, there have been numerous reports of strange happenings, otherworldly whispers, and ghostly sightings within the hallowed walls of the Basilica. The spectral stories and legends that have emerged from this sacred site have intrigued and mystified generations of visitors, drawing them to the iconic Venetian landmark in search of answers.

One of the most enduring tales of the supernatural at St. Mark's Basilica revolves around the apparition of a mysterious hooded figure, often sighted in the dimly lit corners of the cathedral. The figure, described by witnesses as cloaked in a flowing black robe, is said to be a harbinger of misfortune or death, appearing to those who are destined to meet a tragic end. This enigmatic entity, known as the Black Monk, has been the subject of numerous accounts, with visitors claiming to have encountered the spectral figure while wandering the cathedral's shadowy recesses.

In one such account, a Venetian nobleman, visiting the Basilica to offer prayers for a recently deceased family member, described coming face to face with the Black Monk. As he stood before the ornate tomb of the Doge, a former ruler of Venice, the nobleman claimed that the apparition materialised before him, its features obscured by the shadows of the hood that enshrouded its face. The encounter, which lasted only a few seconds, left the nobleman shaken and bewildered. In the days that followed, the nobleman suffered a series of misfortunes that ultimately led to his financial ruin and social disgrace.

The Black Monk is not the only mysterious apparition that has been reported within the walls of St. Mark's Basilica. In the cathedral's famed Pala d'Oro, a golden altarpiece adorned with precious gems and enamelwork, there have been accounts of a ghostly figure appearing amidst the shimmering mosaics. Known as the Golden Lady, this enigmatic spirit is said to be the restless soul of a young woman who was entombed within the cathedral's walls during the Middle Ages.

The story of the Golden Lady is a tragic one. According to legend, she was a beautiful and virtuous noblewoman who was engaged to be married to a powerful Venetian lord. However, the lord's unscrupulous rivals, driven by jealousy and greed, conspired to tarnish her reputation by spreading false rumours of her infidelity. Heartbroken and dishonoured, the young woman sought refuge within the Basilica, where she spent her remaining days in prayer and penance. Upon her death, she was interred within the cathedral, her final resting place concealed behind the opulent Pala d'Oro.

Over the centuries, numerous visitors to St. Mark's Basilica have claimed to witness the spectral figure of the Golden Lady, her ethereal form seeming to shimmer in the dim light of the cathedral. Her ghostly presence has been described as a manifestation of her undying love for the city of Venice and her desire to protect its sacred treasures from harm. In one notable account, a group of thieves who had broken into the Basilica to steal the precious relics and artefacts were thwarted by the sudden appearance of the Golden Lady. The apparition's otherworldly aura filled the would-be robbers with terror, causing them to flee the scene in haste.

In addition to these two prominent apparitions, St. Mark's Basilica is also known for its numerous accounts of inexplicable phenomena and supernatural occurrences. From disembodied voices echoing through the cathedral's vast chambers to unexplained cold spots and the overwhelming sense of an unseen presence, the stories that have emerged from the Basilica's hallowed halls are as varied as they are fascinating.

One such account involves a choir of ghostly voices that have been heard emanating from the Basilica's choir loft. Numerous visitors have reported hearing the haunting strains of sacred hymns, sung in perfect harmony by an unseen choir. In some cases, the ethereal music is said to be accompanied by the faint scent of incense, as if the spirits of long-dead clergy were still conducting their sacred rites within the cathedral's walls.

In another instance, a group of tourists exploring the Basilica's crypts were startled to discover a set of mysterious footprints that appeared to lead into a solid wall. The footprints, which seemed to be those of a child, were visible only for a few moments before vanishing entirely. The origin of these ghostly footprints remains a mystery, with some speculating that they could be the manifestation of a long-forgotten tragedy that unfolded within the crypts of St. Mark's Basilica.

While the enigmatic apparitions and supernatural occurrences within St. Mark's Basilica have attracted much attention and intrigue, the true nature of these phenomena remains shrouded in mystery. Are they the manifestations of restless spirits, forever bound to the sacred site that has been their eternal home? Or do they represent the lingering echoes of a past steeped in tragedy, devotion, and the inexorable passage of time?

Regardless of the explanation, the tales of the supernatural that continue to emerge from St. Mark's Basilica serve as a testament to the enduring allure of the unknown. For those who venture within the cathedral's majestic walls, the possibility of encountering the enigmatic spirits of Venice's storied past adds an undeniable element of mystique and wonder to the experience.

As we explore the world of haunted churches and sacred sites, St. Mark's Basilica stands as a compelling example of the inexplicable mysteries that continue to captivate the human imagination. In the end, perhaps it is not the answers that we seek, but rather the questions that these haunting tales inspire, that drive our endless fascination with the realm of the supernatural.

The Restless Dead of St. George's Church

In the heart of London, where the bustling metropolis gives way to quiet corners and centuries-old streets, stands a testament to the city's rich and storied past. St. George's Church, an architectural marvel that has weathered the passage of time, stands proudly as a symbol of resilience and faith. While the church's magnificent façade captivates the eyes of visitors, the secrets that lie within its walls and beneath its floors are the subject of whispered tales and eerie legends. In this chapter, we will delve into the mysteries of St. George's Church, unearthing the history of this sacred site and the paranormal phenomena that have come to define its haunted reputation.

The origins of St. George's Church date back to the early 18th century when the structure was built in response to the growing needs of London's expanding population. Designed by renowned architect Nicholas Hawksmoor, the church is a masterpiece of

English Baroque style, boasting an imposing exterior and an ornate interior adorned with intricate carvings and stonework. Over the years, St. George's Church has borne witness to countless moments in history, from the turmoil of the Great Fire of London to the devastation wrought by the Blitz during World War II. Despite the ravages of time, the church has endured, serving as a sanctuary for generations of worshippers who have sought solace within its hallowed walls.

Yet, it is beneath the church's opulent exterior that the true mysteries of St. George's lie. Concealed beneath the flagstones of the church's nave lies an extensive network of crypts and vaults, where the remains of the deceased have been interred for centuries. It is within these dark, labyrinthine chambers that the restless spirits of St. George's Church are said to dwell, forever bound to the sacred site that has been their eternal resting place.

Stories of ghostly encounters and supernatural occurrences within the crypts of St. George's Church have circulated for generations, with numerous eyewitnesses reporting encounters with apparitions, inexplicable cold spots, and the overwhelming sensation of an unseen presence. Among the most famous of these spectral residents is the tormented spirit of a woman who has come to be known as the White Lady. Clad in a flowing white gown, her anguished visage a testament to her eternal sorrow, the White Lady is said to roam the crypts, her restless spirit forever seeking solace in the dark recesses of the church.

The tragic tale of the White Lady is steeped in the annals of London's history, her ill-fated life a testament to the harsh realities of the city's past. Born to a prominent family in the late 18th century, the young woman's privileged upbringing masked a life of torment and abuse at the hands of her cruel and domineering father. Desperate to escape her dire circumstances, she sought refuge in the arms of a young man who worked in her father's household. Their illicit love affair, conducted in secret, was a fleeting reprieve from the young woman's suffering.

However, their clandestine romance was ultimately discovered, leading to disastrous consequences for the star-crossed lovers. The young man was banished from the household, while the woman, shamed and disgraced, was forced to marry a much older and equally cruel man chosen by her father. The young woman's life, marked by misery and despair, came to a tragic end within the walls of her marital home, her spirit forever bound to the crypts of St. George's Church, where her remains were interred.

Eyewitness accounts of encounters with the White Lady abound, with many visitors to the crypts describing a sense of overwhelming sadness as they navigate the dimly lit chambers. Some have reported hearing the faint sounds of weeping, echoing through the vaults as if the White Lady's sorrow permeates the very walls that surround her. Others have seen her ghostly figure, drifting through the shadows, her mournful gaze a haunting reminder of her tragic past.

Another infamous apparition that is said to haunt the crypts of St. George's Church is that of a tall, dark figure, clad in the vestments of a clergyman. This enigmatic spectre, known as the Black Monk, is believed to be the spirit of a former vicar who once presided over the church in the early 19th century. A stern and unforgiving man, the vicar was known for his zealous devotion to his faith and his harsh treatment of those who did not adhere to his strict moral code.

Despite his piety, the vicar's life was marred by scandal and tragedy. Rumours of dark deeds and nefarious acts swirled around the man, casting a shadow over his reputation and ultimately leading to his disgrace. Following his death, the vicar's remains were interred within the crypts of St. George's Church, and it is here that his restless spirit is said to dwell, a malevolent presence that strikes fear into the hearts of those who encounter him.

Visitors to the crypts have reported chilling encounters with the Black Monk, describing the sensation of being watched by unseen eyes and the oppressive feeling of a malevolent presence. Some have even witnessed the dark figure himself, his tall, imposing form materialising from the shadows, only to vanish as quickly as he appeared. The ghostly clergyman's presence is a stark contrast to the sorrowful spirit of the White Lady, with many speculating that the Black Monk's lingering malevolence may be a contributing factor to the unrest within the crypts of St. George's Church.

As tales of ghostly encounters and paranormal phenomena within the crypts of St. George's Church continue to captivate the imagination, the historic site has become a mecca for those seeking to experience the supernatural firsthand. While some visitors embark on guided tours of the church's catacombs, others opt to brave the darkness alone, armed with little more than a flashlight and a sense of curiosity. Despite the chilling atmosphere and the eerie legends that surround the crypts, the allure of the unknown draws countless souls to St. George's Church each year, eager to uncover the truth behind the haunted tales.

In addition to the apparitions of the White Lady and the Black Monk, visitors to St. George's Church have reported a myriad of other unexplained occurrences within the crypts. From sudden drops in temperature and inexplicable sounds to fleeting glimpses of spectral figures, the haunted reputation of the church's catacombs continues to grow with each passing year. While sceptics may attribute these phenomena to the power of suggestion or the effects of the crypts' dark and foreboding atmosphere, the sheer volume of eyewitness accounts lends credence to the belief that something otherworldly lurks within the depths of St. George's Church.

The haunted crypts of St. George's Church offer a chilling glimpse into the darker side of London's storied past. From the tragic tale of the White Lady to the sinister presence of the Black Monk, the spirits that dwell within the church's catacombs serve as a stark reminder of the city's rich and often turbulent history.

Afterword

As we conclude our journey through the hallowed halls and sacred grounds of the world's most haunted churches and sacred sites, we are left with a deeper understanding of the mysteries that lurk within these ancient edifices. These stories have taken us across continents and through centuries, revealing a rich tapestry of human experience, tragedy, and the supernatural. Through the eyes of those who have encountered the spirits that dwell within these hallowed grounds, we have glimpsed a world that defies explanation and beckons us to explore further.

Throughout "Haunted Churches and Sacred Sites: Spirits Among the Pews," we have seen that these locations are not simply repositories of supernatural phenomena; they are also rich with history and human emotion. From the mournful spectre of the Weeping Lady of St. Nicholas Church to the tragic love story that haunts St. Olaf's in Estonia, these tales have illuminated the enduring power of human emotion – love, sorrow, fear, and hope – to transcend the boundaries of life and death. These stories serve as a poignant reminder that, while our understanding of the world may be limited, the depth of human experience knows no bounds.

The ghostly tales and paranormal encounters that we have explored in this book have been drawn from a wide array of sources, including historical records, firsthand accounts, and oral traditions. It is important to remember that these accounts, while undoubtedly compelling, represent only a fraction of the stories that have been passed down through generations. For every chilling tale we have recounted here, countless others remain untold, waiting to be discovered by those with the curiosity and courage to delve into the unknown.

As we reflect on the stories contained within this volume, it is worth considering the broader implications of our fascination with the supernatural. Why are we so drawn to the mysterious, the eerie, and the unexplained? For some, the allure of the unknown may be rooted in a desire to explore the limits of our understanding – to push beyond the boundaries of what we know and confront the mysteries that lie just out of reach. For others, the supernatural may provide a means of grappling with our deepest fears and anxieties, allowing us to confront the unknown in a controlled and contained manner.

Regardless of the reasons that drive us to seek out the supernatural, our fascination with haunted churches and sacred sites is a testament to the enduring power of the human imagination. These stories, passed down through generations and across cultures, have captivated our collective consciousness, giving rise to a thriving subculture of paranormal enthusiasts, ghost hunters, and armchair explorers. For those who seek to understand the world beyond our comprehension, these tales offer a tantalising glimpse into the uncharted realms that lie just beyond the veil.

As we close the pages of "Haunted Churches and Sacred Sites: Spirits Among the Pews," it is our hope that this exploration of the supernatural has not only entertained and enthralled but has also inspired a sense of curiosity and wonder. These stories serve as a reminder that the world is a far more mysterious and complex place than we often give it credit for, and that there is much that remains to be discovered. For those brave enough to venture into the shadows, the journey has only just begun.

In the spirit of continued exploration, we encourage our readers to seek out their own encounters with the supernatural, whether that be through visiting haunted churches and sacred sites, conducting their own paranormal investigations, or simply delving deeper into the rich history and folklore that surrounds these enigmatic locations. The world is a vast and mysterious place, and the spirits among the pews are but one small facet of the endless wonders that await discovery.

As we part ways, we leave you with a quote from the renowned paranormal investigator and author, Hans Holzer, who once said, "Ghosts are a reminder that the past is not really dead but is very much alive." With these words in mind, we invite you to continue your exploration of the haunted and the holy, the eerie and the enigmatic, the spectral and the sacred. May your journey be filled with wonder, discovery, and perhaps even a few spine-tingling encounters with the spirits that dwell within the shadows of our world.

It has been our privilege to guide you through these chilling tales and mysterious phenomena. We are grateful for your curiosity and your courage in joining us on this journey into the unknown. As we part ways, we wish you a life filled with adventure, wisdom, and an ever-present sense of awe at the mysteries that surround us. May the spirits among the pews continue to whisper their stories to those who are willing to listen, and may the haunted churches and sacred sites of our world continue to inspire and captivate the imaginations of generations to come.

Farewell, fellow explorer, and may your path be ever guided by the light of truth and the thrill of discovery.

Thank you for buying this book!

For more books in this series search "Lee Brickley" on Amazon.

Printed in Great Britain
by Amazon